ORIENTAL SEAFOOD

CHARMAINE SOLOMON

HAMLYN

Published 1993 by Hamlyn Australia
a part of Reed Books Australia
22 Salmon Street, Port Melbourne, Victoria 3207
a division of Reed International Books Australia Pty Ltd

Photographs by Reg Morrison
Styling by Margaret Alcock
Food cooked by Jill Pavey, Romany de Silva
China: 'Nantucket' by Waterford Wedgwood Australia Limited.
Ceramic bowls from Made in Japan, Neutral Bay, NSW.
Typeset by Midland Typesetters in 9½/12pt Berkeley Old Style Book
Produced in Hong Kong by Mandarin Offset

National Library of Australia
cataloguing-in-publication data:

Solomon, Charmaine.
Oriental seafood.

Includes index.
ISBN 0 947334 629.

1. Cookery (Seafood). 2. Cookery, Oriental. I. Title. (Series: Asian cooking library).

641.692

Introduction

This book has many classic seafood favourites—the famous Tom Yum Goong (Hot Sour Prawn Soup) of Thailand, Chilli Crabs and Prawn Laksa of Singapore, Cantonese Crayfish with Ginger, and Fried Crab in Black Bean Sauce to name a few.

The recipes are presented according to seafood types. Hence appetising crab dishes can be found under crustaceans, mouth-watering mussel or oyster dishes under molluscs. The fish section is again divided according to how you buy your fish—whole, steaks or fillets. Recipes like Fish and Prawn Rolls that use more than one type of seafood can be found under mixed seafood.

Visiting a large fish market is an educational experience. Each time I find a variety which is new to me. I have specified fish for various recipes, but also give choices of other fish of the same type. If you are unsure, ask your fishmonger which of those in season answer to the description.

Take an insulated bag with a couple of frozen ice blocks in it when you shop, so that the seafood comes home in prime condition. Store it in the refrigerator for no longer than a day or two—Seafood should be cooked and eaten as soon as possible.

Crustaceans

To enjoy crab or lobster at their best, try to buy them live, despatch them speedily and cook them immediately. The preferred method of despatch is severing the spinal cord by plunging a skewer or sharp knife into the brain, but this method needs precision to avoid cruelty.

I am the first to admit to cowardice about such matters and take the soft option—cold-induced anaesthesia. From what I have read on the subject, it seems the most humane method is to place the crustaceans (wrapped in paper or plastic) in the freezer for 20 to 30 minutes so that they lose consciousness. Some authorities say they can then be dropped into boiling water for a few minutes, not long enough to cook them through, but long enough to ensure they are dead. It can be unnerving to see the legs moving while in the pot, but this is due to tissues contracting in the heat.

Remember to remove and discard the gills (grey feathery tissue under the top shell or carapace of crabs) and stomach bag before adding to the recipe.

If the crustaceans you buy are not alive, be guided by the smell. Avoid crustaceans with a strong ammonia-like odour. Even when cooked, they should be given the odour test. Also the flesh should be firm and sweet, not soft or strong-tasting. If you have any doubts at all about their freshness, leave them off your menu.

A favourite at Chinese restaurants when price is no object. Australian restaurants usually serve crayfish or rock lobster rather than true lobster. Guard against overcooking or the flesh will be tough.

Steamed Crayfish with Ginger and Black Beans

Serves 2

- *1 live crayfish or uncooked lobster tail*
- *1 teaspoon finely chopped garlic*
- *1 teaspoon finely chopped ginger*
- *2 teaspoons salted black beans, rinsed*
- *1 tablespoon light soy sauce*
- *1 tablespoon oriental sesame oil*
- *2 spring onions cut into fine shreds*
- *1 tablespoon peanut oil*

Drop crayfish into boiling water for 1 minute or put into freezer for 20 to 30 minutes to immobilise it. Chop head from body, cut body in half lengthways and chop into sections. Put onto a heatproof plate, place in a steamer or on a trivet to hold it above level of water. Mix garlic, ginger, black beans, soy sauce and sesame oil and pour over crayfish. Cover and steam over boiling water for 10 minutes. Remove from heat and sprinkle with shreds of spring onion.

Heat peanut oil until very hot and pour over crayfish so it sizzles. Serve at once.

Singapore Chilli Crab

Serves 4

- *2 medium size live crabs*
- *4 tablespoons peanut oil*
- *2 teaspoons finely chopped garlic*
- *2 teaspoons finely chopped ginger*
- *2 teaspoons chopped red chillies*
- *¼ cup tomato sauce*
- *¼ cup chilli sauce*
- *1 tablespoon sugar*
- *1 tablespoon light soy sauce*
- *½ teaspoon salt*

Put crabs in freezer for 20 to 30 minutes to immobilise them. Remove top shell and feather-like tissue under it. Chop bodies in two (4 if they are large) and detach large claws. Scrub any algae from shells. Crack claws so flavours can penetrate.

Heat oil in a wok and fry pieces of crab quickly, turning them until they become red. Remove from wok and fry garlic and ginger for a few seconds until aromatic. Add chillies and remaining ingredients with ½ cup water. Return pieces of crab and let them simmer in sauce for 5 minutes. Serve with steamed white rice. If using cooked crab, clean as described but only heat through in sauce—it is unnecessary to deep-fry. Reduce oil to 1 tablespoon.

There is a way of removing the sandy intestinal tract of prawns without removing the shell, which makes this dish doubly enjoyable. When eating prawns, tackle them with the fingers as they do in Singapore.

Singapore Prawns in Shell

Serves 4

- *500 g (1 lb) large, raw tiger prawns*
- *3 tablespoons peanut oil*
- *2 spring onions cut in short lengths*
- *2 red chillies, sliced*
- *1 tablespoon shredded fresh ginger*
- *2 teaspoons finely chopped garlic*
- *2 tablespoons dry sherry*
- *2 tablespoons light soy sauce*
- *1 tablespoon sugar*
- *2 teaspoons oriental sesame oil*

Make a small incision in each prawn just above tail segment and snip dark vein. From just below the head find other end of vein and carefully draw out whole length. Wash prawns, leaving entire shell on. Dry on paper towels.

Heat wok, add peanut oil. When oil is very hot, add prawns and stir-fry on high heat until they change colour. Add spring onions, chillies, ginger and garlic and fry for 30 seconds. Add remaining ingredients and bring to the boil, turning prawns in the sauce constantly for 1 minute. Serve at once.

Thai Hot Sour Prawn Soup

Serves 6

- *1 kg (2 lb) raw prawns*
- *1 tablespoon oil*
- *8 cups chicken stock*
- *salt to taste*
- *2 stalks lemon grass, bruised or 4 strips thinly peeled lemon rind*
- *4 kaffir lime leaves*
- *4 fresh red chillies*
- *2 tablespoons fish sauce*
- *lime or lemon juice to taste*
- *2 tablespoons chopped coriander leaves*
- *4 spring onions, including green tops, chopped*

Shell and devein prawns, reserving heads and shells. Wash prawn heads and set aside to drain. Heat oil in a saucepan and fry heads and shells until they turn pink. Add 8 cups chicken stock or hot water, salt, lemon grass or rind, kaffir lime leaves and 3 of the chillies left whole. Bring to the boil, cover and simmer for 20 minutes. Strain stock, return to pan and bring to the boil. Add prawns and simmer for about 3 minutes, or just until prawns are cooked. Stir in fish sauce and lime or lemon juice to taste. The soup should have a pronounced acidic flavour. Serve sprinkled with remaining chilli sliced, coriander leaves and spring onions.

One of those cross-culture dishes that appears on many Asian menus and reflects the Western influence while keeping the spicy touch of Asia.

Baked Devilled Crab

Serves 2

- *2 large mud crabs*
- *2 tablespoons butter*
- *¼ cup finely chopped spring onions*
- *2 fresh green chillies, seeded and sliced*
- *2 tablespoons plain flour*
- *1 cup milk*
- *2 teaspoons finely chopped fresh dill*
- *2 teaspoons prepared hot English mustard*
- *2 teaspoons Worcestershire Sauce*
- *pinch of chilli powder*
- *2 eggs*
- *salt and pepper to taste*
- *2 tablespoons breadcrumbs*
- *2 teaspoons butter*

Buy cooked crabs or boil them. Remove top shell carefully, scrub well and set aside. Discard feather-like tissue under shell. Pick all flesh from body and legs of crabs and discard any bits of shell or cartilage.

Melt butter in a small saucepan and gently cook spring onions and chillies until soft. Add flour and cook, stirring, for a minute or two without browning. Add milk and stir until mixture comes to the boil and is smooth and thick. Remove from heat, add dill, mustard, Worcestershire Sauce, chilli powder and egg yolks. Mix in crabmeat and season with salt and pepper to taste, then fold in stiffly beaten egg whites.

Fill crab shells with mixture, sprinkle with breadcrumbs and dot with small dabs of butter. Bake in a moderate oven, 180°C (350°F), for about 20 minutes or until golden brown. Or if you prefer, divide mixture among 4 ramekins and bake for about 15 minutes.

Note This dish will serve 4 as an appetiser.

Sri Lankan Prawn Curry

Serves 6

- *750 g (1½ lb) raw prawns*
- *1 medium onion, chopped finely*
- *2 large cloves garlic, chopped finely*
- *2 teaspoons finely grated fresh ginger*
- *1 small stick cinnamon*
- *½ teaspoon cummin seeds*
- *4 curry leaves*
- *small piece lemon grass stem, bruised or 2 strips lemon rind*
- *1 strip pandan leaf*
- *½ teaspoon ground turmeric*
- *1 teaspoon chilli powder*
- *2 teaspoons paprika*
- *salt to taste*
- *1 cup canned coconut milk*
- *1 tablespoon lime or lemon juice*

Wash prawns and remove heads, but leave rest of shells intact. Carefully draw out vein (see Singapore Prawns in Shell, p. 4)

Put all ingredients, except prawns and lime juice, into a saucepan. Stir in 1 cup water and bring slowly to simmering point. Simmer, uncovered, 10 minutes. Add prawns and lime juice and stir. Simmer a further 10 minutes. Add more salt and lime juice if necessary. Serve with boiled rice.

Burmese curries have a very special flavour which comes from long, slow cooking of onions, garlic and ginger rather than heavy spicing. In fact relatively few spices in very small amounts are used. The use of sesame oil also contributes a distinctive flavour.

Burmese Prawn Curry

Serves 4

- *500 g (1 lb) raw prawns*
- *1 large onion, chopped roughly*
- *4 cloves garlic*
- *1 teaspoon finely grated fresh ginger*
- *½ teaspoon ground turmeric*
- *¼ teaspoon chilli powder*
- *¼ teaspoon ground fennel*
- *2 tablespoons peanut oil*
- *1 tablespoon oriental sesame oil*
- *salt to taste*
- *2 tablespoons chopped fresh coriander leaves*
- *2 tablespoons chopped green of spring onions*

Shell and devein prawns. Place onion, garlic and ginger in a blender and grind to a purée. Mix in turmeric, chilli powder and fennel.

Heat peanut and sesame oils in a saucepan until very hot. Carefully add puréed ingredients—the oil will sputter violently. Lower heat and stir ingredients into oil. Add salt to taste. Cover pan and simmer for about 15 minutes, lifting lid frequently to stir and scrape base of pan with a wooden spoon. If mixture fries too rapidly, add a little water as necessary and stir well. When ready, onion will be soft and transparent, mixture will have a rich red-brown colour and mellow aroma, and oil will show around edge of mass.

Add prawns and stir well. Sprinkle with fresh coriander leaves, then cover pan and cook for 10 minutes or until prawns are done. Remove from heat and stir in spring onions. Serve hot with rice.

The lime leaves used in this recipe (as in most Thai recipes) are those of the kaffir lime. Its intense citrus fragrance is unique.

Chilli Prawn with Lime

Serves 4 to 6

- *500 g (1 lb) medium raw prawns*
- *2 teaspoons finely chopped fresh ginger*
- *1 tablespoon fish sauce*
- *2 teaspoons palm sugar or brown sugar*
- *4 spring onions, sliced diagonally*
- *4 fresh red chillies*
- *2 teaspoons finely chopped fresh or frozen galangal*
- *1 tablespoon chopped lemon grass*
- *1 small onion, chopped finely*
- *1 tablespoon Pepper and Coriander Paste (see p. 10)*
- *2 tablespoons peanut oil*
- *¾ cup canned coconut milk*
- *1 teaspoon rice flour*
- *salt to taste*
- *finely shredded fresh kaffir lime leaves (see Note) and fresh red chilli*

Shell prawns, but leave tail segment intact. Carefully devein and using a sharp knife slit each prawn in half from the top, for about a third of its length. Place in a bowl and mix in ginger, fish sauce, sugar and spring onions. Marinate for 10 minutes.

Split chillies and discard seeds for less heat. Purée in a blender with galangal, lemon grass, onion and Pepper and Coriander Paste, scraping down sides of blender as necessary.

Heat oil in a wok or frying pan, add paste mixture and stir-fry until fragrant. Add prawns with their marinade and cook until they change colour—about 3 minutes—turning constantly. Remove pan from heat.

Mix 2 tablespoons of the coconut milk with rice flour. Heat remaining coconut milk in a small saucepan and as it comes to the boil stir in rice flour mixture and continue stirring for a few seconds until sauce thickens. Add salt to taste and pour immediately into the centre of a serving plate or bowl. Place prawns on sauce and sprinkle with lime leaves (or rind) and fresh chilli.

Note If fresh lime leaves are unavailable, use shreds of lime or lemon rind in preference to dried kaffir lime leaves.

Pepper and Coriander Paste

Makes about 1 cup

- *1 tablespoon chopped garlic*
- *2 teaspoons salt*
- *1 tablespoon whole black peppercorns*
- *2 cups coarsely chopped fresh coriander, including roots*
- *4 tablespoons lemon juice*

Crush garlic with salt to a smooth paste. Roast peppercorns in a dry pan for about 2 minutes. Finely chop coriander roots, leaves and stems. Mix all ingredients with lemon juice and grind in a blender, adding a little water if necessary. Or use mortar and pestle and pound to a paste.

Lobster and Coconut Salad

Serves 2

- *1 medium-size cooked rock lobster*
- *1 teaspoon sugar*
- *1/3 cup fresh lime juice*
- *1 small purple onion, sliced finely*
- *3 red chillies, seeded and sliced*
- *1 teaspoon rice flour*
- *1 cup canned coconut milk*
- *1 tablespoon fish sauce*
- *2 fresh kaffir lime leaves, shredded*

With a sharp knife cut into lobster from underneath, removing meat from tail. Cut across into rounds. Reserve claws and legs. Place lobster rounds in a bowl. Stir sugar into lime juice until dissolved, then pour over lobster. Add a few slices of onion and half the chillies. Gently mix and set aside.

Mix rice flour with 1 tablespoon coconut milk. Heat remaining coconut milk in a small saucepan. Stir in rice flour mixture and cook until slightly thickened. Pour into a bowl to cool. Drain liquid from lobster and stir it into coconut milk; add fish sauce. Pour coconut milk dressing over base of serving dish. Arrange lobster slices on top. Pile remaining onion and chilli slices in centre and garnish with kaffir lime leaves and lobster claws and legs. Serve cold as an entrée.

Unless you have been brought up to manage crab with chopsticks, the best way to eat this popular dish is with your fingers so none of the delicious crabmeat is missed. Serve with steamed white rice to soak up the salty sauce.

Fried Crab in Black Bean Sauce

Serves 4

- *1 large, uncooked crab*
- *1 tablespoon salted black beans*
- *1 tablespoon light soy sauce*
- *1 tablespoon dry sherry*
- *1 teaspoon sugar*
- *2 large cloves garlic, crushed*
- *¼ cup peanut oil*
- *1 teaspoon finely chopped fresh ginger*
- *2 teaspoons cornflour*
- *3 spring onions, chopped*
- *1 egg, slightly beaten*

Thoroughly scrub crab under cold, running water until shell is clean. Remove and discard hard top shell and fibrous tissue underneath. Discard stomach bag attached to shell below the eyes. Chop body of crab into 6 pieces with a heavy cleaver. Leave legs attached but detach large claws from body. Crack shell of claws to allow sauce to penetrate.

Briefly rinse black beans in a strainer under cold water, drain and mash well with soy sauce, sherry, sugar and half the garlic.

Heat oil in a wok and fry remaining garlic and ginger until they begin to turn golden, then raise heat and stir-fry crab pieces, turning constantly until shells are bright red—about 4 minutes. Remove crab from wok. Add black bean mixture to oil and fry for 1 minute. Stir in 2/3 cup hot water, return crab and stir well. Cover and cook for 3 minutes or until flesh is white and opaque. Remove crab to a hot serving dish.

Mix cornflour with 1 tablespoon cold water and stir into sauce until it boils and thickens. Add spring onions and egg and continue stirring just until egg sets. Pour over crab and serve immediately with steamed white rice.

Spiced Rice with Prawns

Serves 4

- *1½ cups basmati or other long grain rice*
- *1 tablespoon ghee*
- *1 tablespoon peanut oil*
- *500 g (1 lb) raw prawns, shelled and deveined*
- *1 medium onion, sliced finely*
- *4 cloves garlic, chopped finely*
- *1 teaspoon finely grated fresh ginger*
- *1 small stick cinnamon*
- *3 whole cloves*
- *4 cardamom pods, bruised*
- *1 teaspoon Garam Masala (see p. 84)*
- *2 fresh chillies, seeded and sliced*
- *1 teaspoon salt or to taste*
- *seedless cucumber and coriander leaves*

Wash rice if necessary and set aside to drain for at least 30 minutes. Heat ghee and oil in a heavy saucepan and fry prawns quickly, stirring, just until they change colour. Remove from pan with slotted spoon and set aside. Put onion, garlic, ginger and whole spices into pan and fry for a few minutes, stirring frequently. Stir in rice and fry until all grains are coated with ghee. Add Garam Masala, chillies, salt and 3 cups hot water. Stir and bring quickly to boil. Reduce heat to very low, cover pan tightly (place a sheet of foil between lid and pan if lid is loose) and cook for 10 minutes. Add prawns, replace cover and cook for a further 5 minutes. Transfer to serving plate. Garnish with thin slices of cucumber and sprinkle with coriander leaves.

Served as an accompaniment to rice and curries, this Indonesian dish is sometimes described as a sambal *as it is rather hot and spicy.*

Fried Prawns with Coconut Milk

Serves 4

- *500 g (1 lb) raw prawns*
- *2 tablespoons peanut oil*
- *1 onion, chopped finely*
- *2 fresh green chillies, seeded and chopped*
- *3 cloves garlic, chopped finely*
- *1 teaspoon finely chopped galangal*
- *1 teaspoon sambal ulek or more to taste*
- *2/3 cup canned coconut milk*
- *salt to taste*
- *1 teaspoon palm sugar or brown sugar*

Shell and devein prawns. Heat oil in a wok or frying pan and fry onion, chillies, garlic and galangal over low heat, stirring occasionally, until onions are soft and golden—about 5 minutes.

Stir in sambal ulek and fry for a few seconds. Add prawns and stir-fry until they change colour. Stir in coconut milk, salt and sugar. Simmer, uncovered, over low heat until liquid thickens and oil starts to separate.

Long Soup with Prawns

Serves 6

- *8 dried shiitake (Chinese) mushrooms*
- *500 g (1 lb) medium raw prawns*
- *250 g (8 oz) fine egg noodles*
- *6 cups prawn or chicken stock*
- *1 teaspoon oriental sesame oil*
- *salt to taste*
- *3 stalks Chinese broccoli (gai larn)*
- *2 tablespoons peanut oil*
- *1 small clove garlic, crushed*
- *1 teaspoon finely grated fresh ginger*
- *1 tablespoon light soy sauce*
- *coriander sprigs*

Put mushrooms in a bowl, cover with hot water and soak for 30 minutes. Simmer mushrooms in stock 15 minutes. Discard stems, cut caps into fine slices. Shell and devein prawns. Soak noodles in hot water to loosen strands, drain in colander, drop into lightly salted boiling water and cook until just tender. Rinse with cold water and drain.

Bring stock to the boil, add noodles and stir in sesame oil and salt to taste. Remove from heat and leave while cooking broccoli and prawns. Cut broccoli stems diagonally into very thin slices. Heat peanut oil in wok and stir-fry broccoli on high heat for 30 seconds or until it turns a brilliant emerald green. Remove to a plate. Add garlic and ginger and fry gently for a few seconds. Toss in prawns and cook over high heat, stirring constantly, until they change colour—about 3 minutes. Stir in sliced mushrooms and soy sauce. Remove from heat.

Ladle hot noodles and soup into individual bowls. Place a portion of prawns, mushroom slices and broccoli on top. Garnish with small sprigs of coriander.

For simplicity it is hard to beat steamed prawns served with a dipping sauce. Remember the prawns must be fresh, not frozen.

Steamed Prawns

Serves 4

- *750 g (1½ lb) raw, medium-size prawns*
- *salt*
- *2 tablespoons light soy sauce*
- *2 tablespoons dark soy sauce*
- *2 teaspoons finely grated fresh ginger*
- *2 teaspoons finely chopped spring onion*
- *1 teaspoon finely chopped red chilli*

Rub prawns well with coarse salt. Rinse in a colander under cold water, then immerse prawns in a bowl of iced water for 10 to 15 minutes. Meanwhile combine sauces, divide in half and mix ginger and spring onion into one portion, the chilli into the other.

Bring a wok of water to the boil, place prawns in a steaming basket or wire strainer and steam over high heat for 7 or 8 minutes, just until prawns turn bright red. Put prawns on serving plate and serve at once with dipping sauces.

Rice Vermicelli with Prawns

Serves 4

- *250 g (8 oz) rice vermicelli*
- *6 leaves mustard cabbage (gai choy)*
- *2 cloves garlic, crushed*
- *1 teaspoon finely grated fresh ginger*
- *1 tablespoon dry sherry*
- *salt to taste*
- *1 tablespoon soy sauce*
- *½ cup prawn stock*
- *3 tablespoons peanut oil*
- *250 g (8 oz) raw prawns, shelled and deveined*

Soak vermicelli in hot water for 10 minutes, then drain in colander. Wash cabbage and remove tough ends of leaves. Slice stems across into thin strips. Mix garlic, ginger, sherry, salt, soy sauce and stock in a bowl.

Heat a wok, add oil and swirl, add prawns and stir-fry, tossing until they change colour. Transfer to a bowl. Let oil regain its heat, add cabbage stems and stir-fry for 1 minute. Stir in stock mixture and cook for 1 minute more. Add rice vermicelli to wok and toss until heated through. Return prawns, tossing until well mixed. Serve immediately.

Which Asian food enthusiast visiting Singapore has not fallen under the spell of this spicy soup known as laksa*? It is a one-dish meal of noodles, vegetables, seafood and coconut milk.*

Spicy Prawn Soup

Serves 6 to 8

- *500 g (1 lb) raw prawns*
- *1 tablespoon peanut oil*
- *salt to taste*
- *375 g (12 oz) rice vermicelli*
- *250 g (8 oz) fresh bean sprouts*
- *4 small, seedless green cucumbers*
- *small bunch fresh laksa leaves (see Note)*

Soup

- *6 large, dried red chillies*
- *2 teaspoons dried shrimp paste (blachan)*
- *2 medium onions, roughly chopped*
- *2 teaspoons galangal powder or chopped galangal in brine*
- *2 stems lemon grass, finely sliced or thinly peeled rind of 1 lemon*
- *4 tablespoons peanut oil*
- *1 teaspoon ground turmeric*
- *1 tablespoon ground coriander*
- *2 cups canned coconut milk*
- *sambal ulek*
- *fresh limes*

Wash prawns and remove shells and heads, reserving them for stock. Devein prawns.

Heat 1 tablespoon of oil in a large saucepan, add prawn shells and heads and fry, stirring, until they turn red. Add 2 litres water and simmer, covered, for about 30 minutes. Strain stock and season to taste with salt. Discard shells and heads.

Place rice vermicelli in a bowl and cover with very hot water. Leave to soak for 10 minutes, then drain. Pinch any straggly tails off bean sprouts, wash well and drain in a colander. Wash cucumbers and cut into matchstick strips. Shred laksa leaves finely.

Soup Remove stems from dry chillies and shake out seeds. Soak chillies in hot water for 10 minutes. Place chillies with shrimp paste, onions, galangal, lemon grass or rind in a blender. Blend to a purée, adding a little of the chilli soaking water.

Heat 3 tablespoons of the oil in a heavy saucepan and fry purée, stirring constantly, until fragrant and browned. Add turmeric and coriander and stir for 1 minute more. Add strained stock and simmer 10 minutes. Before serving add coconut milk mixed with 4 cups water, adding more salt to taste if required. Heat remaining tablespoon of oil in a small pan and stir-fry prawns just until they change colour—about 2 minutes. Season with salt to taste.

Serve soup in large bowls, topping each serve with bean sprouts, cucumber strips, a few prawns and shreds of laksa leaf. Offer sambal ulek and fresh lime wedges in small bowls for those who like extra piquancy in their meal.

Note Laksa leaves are sold in many countries as Vietnamese mint. Recognise them by the pointed leaves with a distinctive marking and a zingy, tongue-tingling taste.

Prawn Ball Soup

Serves 6

- *500 g (1 lb) raw prawns, shelled and deveined*
- *½ teaspoon finely grated fresh ginger*
- *2 slices soft white bread, crumbed*
- *cornflour*
- *1 teaspoon salt*
- *6 cups prawn or chicken stock*
- *½ teaspoon oriental sesame oil*
- *2 tablespoons finely chopped spring onions*

Chop prawns finely. Mix with ginger, breadcrumbs, 2 teaspoons cornflour and salt. Make balls, simmer in stock. Thicken with 1 tablespoon cornflour. Add sesame oil and spring onions.

Whole Fish

It is much easier to judge whether a fish is truly fresh if bought whole: the fish should be shiny and bright; the eyes clear, not sunken; the gills bright red; the flesh firm (when pressed gently with a fingertip the flesh should not hold an impression); and the smell should be of the sea. Avoid any strong-smelling fish.

Hunan-style Boiled Fish

Serves 4

- *1 x 1 kg (2 lb) ocean perch, pigfish or similar white fish*
- *salt to taste*
- *1 tablespoon peanut oil*
- *1 teaspoon finely grated fresh ginger*
- *2 cloves garlic, chopped finely*
- *8 spring onions, chopped finely*
- *2 teaspoons oriental sesame oil*
- *1 teaspoon chilli sauce*
- *2 tablespoons light soy sauce*
- *shredded lettuce*

Purchase fish scaled and cleaned. Wash fish and trim spines and fins with kitchen scissors. Pour sufficient water into a wok to cover fish, but do not add fish at this point. Add salt, bring water to the boil, then lower fish into it. Cover and return to the boil. Reduce heat and cook for about 8 minutes or until flesh is opaque when tested at thickest point. Remove from liquid with flat wire strainer and drain.

Heat peanut oil and fry ginger, garlic and spring onions very gently, just until soft, but not browned. Remove from heat and stir in sesame oil, chilli and soy sauces until well mixed. Serve fish on shredded lettuce with sauce spooned over.

Poached Fish with Peanuts

Serves 4 to 6

- *1 x 1.5 kg (3 lb) snapper or similar white fish*
- *salt*
- *1 large onion, sliced*
- *2 stalks celery, including tops*
- *1 large carrot, quartered*
- *6 thin slices fresh ginger*
- *½ cup dry sherry*
- *½ teaspoon whole black peppercorns*
- *½ cup peanut oil*
- *½ cup raw peanut halves*
- *60 g (2 oz) fatty roast pork, diced*
- *1 tablespoon dark soy sauce*
- *2 teaspoons oriental sesame oil*
- *2 spring onions, sliced diagonally*

Purchase fish cleaned and scaled. Rub cavity with damp paper towel and coarse salt, then rinse. Trim fins with kitchen scissors. Put sufficient water into wok to cover fish, but don't add fish at this point. Add onion, celery, carrot, ginger, sherry and peppercorns. Bring slowly to the boil and simmer for 5 minutes, then put on fast boil and add fish. When water returns to boil, lower heat and poach for about 8 minutes or until fish is cooked and opaque at the thickest point. Turn heat off, carefully lift fish with two large frying slices and suspend over wok to drain for a few seconds. Transfer to a warm platter.

Heat oil and fry peanuts over medium heat until pale golden. Lift out and drain on paper towel. Pour off remaining oil into a heatproof bowl and set aside. Add pork to wok and stir-fry until crisp. Remove with slotted spoon and set aside. Pour off fat and wipe out wok. Return 3 tablespoons of reserved oil to wok until very hot. Mix soy sauce and sesame oil and spoon over fish. Quickly pour hot oil from wok over the top. Garnish with pork, peanuts and spring onion slices. Serve at once with steamed white rice.

Steamed Fish

Serves 4 to 6

- *1 x 1 kg (2 lb) red emperor, coral trout, snapper or similar white fish*
- *salt*
- *2 tablespoons peanut oil*
- *1 teaspoon finely grated fresh ginger*
- *2 cloves garlic, chopped finely*
- *8 spring onions, chopped finely*
- *2 tablespoons light soy sauce*
- *2 teaspoons oriental sesame oil*
- *1 tablespoon toasted sesame seeds*

Purchase fish scaled and cleaned. Trim fins and spines with kitchen scissors and rub cavity with salt. Rinse and drain. Place on a heatproof plate, cover and steam over boiling water for 15 minutes or until cooked through. Flesh will be opaque when tested at thickest part.

Heat peanut oil in a small pan and fry the ginger, garlic and spring onions over very low heat, until soft but not browned. Remove from heat and stir in soy sauce and sesame oil. Serve fish immediately with sauce spooned over and sprinkled with sesame seeds.

Fish Steamed in Banana Leaves

Serves 4

- *4 small pomfret, sole or John Dory*
- *salt*
- *juice and pulp of 2 limes*
- *1 teaspoon chopped fresh ginger*
- *2 cloves garlic*
- *2 large, fresh green chillies, seeded and chopped*
- *½ cup coriander leaves*
- *1 teaspoon ground coriander seeds*
- *½ teaspoon ground cummin*
- *½ cup fresh grated or desiccated coconut*
- *2 tablespoons oil*
- *2 medium onions, chopped finely*
- *banana leaves or foil*

Purchase fish cleaned and scaled. Rinse, dry and rub with salt. Put lime juice and pulp into blender with ginger, garlic, chillies, fresh and ground coriander, cummin and coconut. Blend until puréed.

Heat oil in pan and fry onions until soft and golden. Add blended mixture and fry, stirring, for a few minutes. Cool. Coat each fish with mixture, spreading some in cavity. Wrap separately in banana leaves or foil and steam over simmering water for 30 minutes, turning once. Serve in leaf parcels.

This dish takes its name from the North Indian clay oven known as a tandoor. As this oven reaches an intense heat, any fish cooked in it will be ready very quickly. You can still achieve a good result by cooking the fish over barbecue coals or under a preheated griller. The marinade traditionally used for tandoori fish gives it a distinctive red colour.

Tandoori Fish

Serves 4

- *1 x 1 kg (2 lb) bream, mullet, trevally, tailor or similar firm-fleshed fish*
- *coarse sea salt*
- *2 cloves garlic, crushed*
- *2 teaspoons finely grated fresh ginger*
- *1 teaspoon ground cummin*
- *1 teaspoon ground coriander*
- *1 teaspoon chilli powder*
- *1 teaspoon ground turmeric*
- *2 teaspoons paprika*
- *salt to taste*
- *lime or lemon juice*
- *3 tablespoons melted ghee*
- *2 teaspoons Garam Masala (see p. 84)*

Buy fish cleaned and scaled with head removed. Clean cavity of fish by rubbing with damp paper towel dipped in salt. Wash fish thoroughly under cold, running water then dry with paper towel. Using a sharp knife cut deep slashes along each side of fish. In a bowl mix garlic, ginger, cummin, coriander, chilli powder, turmeric and paprika with salt to taste and sufficient lime or lemon juice to make a thick paste. Rub marinade over fish, inside cavity and into slashes.

Marinate for at least 1 hour in refrigerator. Run a long metal skewer through fish from head to tail and grill, brushing with melted ghee. It should take 6 to 7 minutes on each side. When fish is almost ready, sprinkle with Garam Masala. Serve with an Indian bread such as naan or parathas.

This dish should be served immediately the fish is cooked, so it is best to prepare the sauce ingredients first and simmer the sauce while the fish is frying.

Fried Fish with Mushroom Sauce

Serves 2 to 3

- *1 x 1 kg (2 lb) snapper, bream or similar white fish*
- *flour, seasoned with salt to taste*
- *oil for frying*
- *fresh coriander sprigs*

Mushroom Sauce

- *8 dried shiitake (Chinese) mushrooms*
- *¼ cup vinegar*
- *4 tablespoons sugar*
- *2 tablespoons soy sauce*
- *1 tablespoon cornflour*
- *2 tablespoons diagonally sliced spring onions*
- *4 tablespoons shredded red ginger*

Purchase fish cleaned and scaled. Trim fins and tail with kitchen scissors and scrub cavity with paper towel dipped in coarse salt. Rinse and dry thoroughly. Using a sharp knife make deep diagonal slashes on each side of fish, forming diamond shapes in flesh.

Dip fish in seasoned flour, dust off excess. Deep-fry in

hot oil, turning to fry both sides until golden brown. Drain on absorbent paper.

Carefully transfer fish to serving dish, spoon Sauce over and serve immediately, garnished with a sprig of fresh coriander if desired.

Mushroom Sauce Soak mushrooms in hot water for 30 minutes, drain, discard stems and cut caps into slices. Put mushroom slices, vinegar, sugar and soy sauce into a small saucepan with ¾ cup water. Bring to the boil and simmer for 15 minutes. Mix cornflour with 1 tablespoon cold water, stir into sauce. Add spring onions and cook, stirring, over medium heat until sauce becomes clear and thick. Remove from heat and stir in shredded ginger.

Spiced Baked Fish

Serves 4

- *1 x 1 kg (2 lb) snapper or coral trout, cleaned and scaled*
- *salt and lime juice*
- *2 tablespoons oil*
- *2 tablespoons finely chopped fresh ginger*
- *3 cloves garlic, finely chopped*
- *1 fresh red chilli, seeded and chopped*
- *½ teaspoon turmeric*
- *2 teaspoons Garam Masala (see p. 84)*
- *1 cup plain yoghurt*
- *1 tablespoon chopped coriander leaves*

Scrub cavity with damp kitchen paper dipped in coarse salt to remove traces of blood. Rinse well. Dry fish on paper towels and sprinkle cavity with salt and lime juice. Heat oil and fry ginger, garlic and chilli until soft. Add spices, fry briefly, cool and stir in yoghurt and coriander. Make slits in flesh, spread marinade over and in cavity. Bake in a greased dish in moderate oven for 35 minutes or until done. Serve hot.

Fish with Ham and Bamboo Shoots

Serves 4

- *6 dried shiitake (Chinese) mushrooms*
- *1 x 1 kg (2 lb) snapper, bream or similar white fish*
- *salt to taste*
- *1 tablespoon light soy sauce*
- *2 teaspoons oriental sesame oil*
- *1 teaspoon sugar*
- *2 tablespoons dry sherry*
- *1 tablespoon finely shredded fresh ginger*
- *¼ cup each matchstick strips of ham and bamboo shoots*
- *2 spring onions, cut into matchstick strips*
- *fresh coriander sprigs*

Soak mushrooms in hot water for 20 minutes. Meanwhile prepare fish. (Make sure fish you buy has been scaled and cleaned.) Wipe with paper towels and rub inside and out with salt. Discard stems from soaked mushrooms, reserve soaking water, and cut caps into thin strips. Put mushroom strips in a small saucepan with soy sauce, sesame oil, sugar and ½ cup of the mushroom water. Bring to the boil, cover and simmer for 10 minutes. Remove mushroom strips from liquid with slotted spoon and add sherry to pan.

Lightly oil a heatproof dish and layer half the strips of mushroom, ginger, bamboo, ham and spring onions over base. Put fish on top and spread remaining strips over surface. Place dish in a steamer over gently boiling water, cover and steam for about 12 minutes, or until fish is cooked—flesh will be opaque when tested at thickest point. Pour sherry mixture on top and serve garnished with coriander sprigs.

Fish with Coconut Sauce

Serves 2

- *1 x 500 g (1 lb) pomfret, sole, John Dory or similar delicate flat fish*
- *1 tablespoon oil*
- *1½ tablespoons Green Curry Paste (see p. 83)*
- *1 teaspoon lime juice*
- *½ cup grated fresh coconut or desiccated coconut*
- *2 tablespoons finely sliced spring onions*
- *2 tablespoons chopped coriander leaves*
- *½ cup canned coconut milk*
- *1 teaspoon fish sauce*
- *1 small green chilli, chopped*
- *cornflour*
- *oil for frying*

Purchase fish cleaned and scaled. With a sharp knife lightly score flesh on each side where it is thickest. Heat oil in a pan and fry Green Curry Paste, stirring constantly, until fragrant. Mix 1 teaspoon of the fried paste with lime juice and half the grated coconut. (If using desiccated coconut you will need to moisten it slightly with water.) Pack into cavity of fish.

Stir remaining coconut, spring onions, coriander, coconut milk, fish sauce and green chilli into fried paste remaining in pan. Add ½ cup water and simmer mixture, stirring, for 5 minutes. Cool slightly, then blend at high speed.

Coat fish in cornflour, dusting off excess. Heat sufficient oil in frying pan for shallow frying and fry fish, first on one side and then the other, turning carefully, until golden brown. Transfer to a serving plate and coat with sauce. Serve remaining sauce separately.

Trout in Piquant Sauce

Serves 4 to 6

- *1 x 1 kg (2 lb) rainbow trout*
- *2 tablespoons cornflour*
- *salt to taste*
- *½ teaspoon five spice powder*
- *2 tablespoons dry sherry*
- *2 tablespoons light soy sauce*
- *2 teaspoons sugar*
- *1 tablespoon rice vinegar or other mild vinegar*
- *1 teaspoon oriental sesame oil*
- *1 cup peanut oil*
- *2 spring onions, chopped*
- *1 clove garlic, chopped finely*
- *2 teaspoons finely chopped fresh ginger*
- *chopped coriander leaves*

Wash and dry fish and make deep diagonal cuts on both sides. Mix cornflour, salt and five spice powder. Coat trout, rubbing into slashes. Mix sherry, soy sauce, sugar, vinegar and sesame oil with ½ cup water, stirring until sugar dissolves.

Heat oil in a wok and slide in fish. Fry over medium heat until browned on one side (about 2 minutes), then turn and fry the other side. Remove fish. Pour off all but 1 tablespoon of oil. Reheat and add spring onions, garlic and ginger; stir-fry for 1 minute without browning. Stir in sherry mixture. Return fish and simmer, covered, over low heat for 5 minutes. Carefully turn fish over and simmer for a further 4 to 5 minutes. Transfer to warmed serving dish and sprinkle with coriander leaves.

Szechwan-style Boiled Fish

Serves 4

- *1 x 1 kg (2 lb) snapper, pearl perch or similar white fish*
- *4 dried shiitake (Chinese) mushrooms*
- *1 tablespoon dry sherry*
- *2 teaspoons chilli bean sauce*
- *2 teaspoons vinegar*
- *½ teaspoon sugar*
- *1 tablespoon peanut oil*
- *1 teaspoon finely grated fresh ginger*
- *1 small clove garlic, crushed*
- *4 spring onions, sliced diagonally*
- *finely sliced, fresh red chilli*

Purchase fish cleaned and scaled. Trim fins and tail with kitchen scissors. With a sharp knife make 3 or 4 diagonal slashes on each side of fish, half-way through to bone. Soak dried mushrooms in hot water for 20 minutes, then discard stems and finely slice caps, reserving water. Mix sherry, chilli bean sauce, vinegar and sugar with 2 tablespoons of reserved mushroom water.

Heat sufficient water in a wok to cover fish and when it comes to a boil, lower fish in, cover and reduce heat. Cook fish with water just simmering for 4 to 5 minutes. Turn off heat and leave covered in water for 15 minutes.

Meanwhile heat peanut oil and fry ginger and garlic over low heat, just until turning golden. Add mushroom and spring onions and fry for 1 minute. Add sherry mixture and bring to the boil. Remove fish with large wire strainer and drain. Transfer to serving dish, pour sauce over and garnish with chilli.

This popular Penang dish has a delicious piquant flavour.

Sour Fish Soup

Serves 4 to 6

- *1 kg (2 lb) jewfish or similar firm white fish including head*
- *2 rounded tablespoons dried tamarind*
- *6 large, dried red chillies*
- *2 stems lemon grass*
- *2 cm (¾ inch) slice fresh turmeric or 1 teaspoon ground*
- *2 slices galangal in brine*
- *2 brown onions, peeled and chopped roughly*
- *1 teaspoon dried shrimp paste*
- *2 tablespoons oil*
- *2 teaspoons palm or brown sugar*
- *1 teaspoon salt or to taste*
- *750 g (1½ lb) fresh rice noodles or 250 g (8 oz) dried*
- *1 white onion, sliced thinly*
- *6 slices half-ripe pineapple*
- *1 small cucumber cut in strips*
- *fresh mint or Vietnamese mint leaves*
- *fresh basil leaves, optional*

Clean and scale fish and simmer in 3 cups water (lightly salted) for 15 minutes or until fish is cooked. Strain and reserve stock. Discard head. Flake half the fish and keep remaining half in large pieces, discarding skin and bones.

Soak and dissolve tamarind pulp in 3 cups hot water, strain through nylon strainer and reserve. Break off stems of chillies, shake out seeds and soak chillies in 1 cup hot water for 10 minutes.

Slice lemon grass finely, scrape skin from turmeric and chop galangal. Combine lemon grass, turmeric and galangal with onions, soaked chillies and shrimp paste in blender or food processor. Add a little water to help blending and process to a purée.

Heat oil in a saucepan and fry purée over low heat, stirring, until cooked and fragrant, about 5 minutes. Add tamarind liquid, bring to simmering point and let it cook for 5 minutes, then stir in sugar, salt, fish stock and flaked fish. Simmer a further 10 minutes. Turn off heat, add larger pieces of fish and keep covered.

Pour boiling water over fresh rice noodles in a colander (or cook dried rice noodles in boiling water 3 minutes or until tender and drain well). Divide noodles among individual bowls, top with sliced onion, pieces of pineapple and cucumber. Pour on fish soup and sprinkle with mint and basil leaves. Serve hot.

Deep-fried Sprats

Serves 4

- *500 g (1 lb) fresh sprats or tiny anchovies*
- *seasoned flour*
- *oil for deep-frying*
- *½ teaspoon salt*
- *½ teaspoon chilli powder*

Remove heads of fish—they are usually too tiny to attempt cleaning the body cavity, but you be the judge, depending on the size of sprats or anchovies available. Dredge in flour, dust off excess and fry immediately in hot oil until golden brown. Lift out on slotted spoon and drain on absorbent paper. Serve at once, sprinkled with salt and chilli powder.

Fillets, Steaks and Cutlets

When buying fish fillets or cutlets as opposed to whole fish, it is harder to determine freshness. The best way to judge is by the smell. The fish should have the sweet, fresh smell of the sea, the flesh should be firm and smooth and the edges not ragged.

Indian-style Fried Fish

Serves 4

- *750 g (1½ lb) tuna, jewfish or kingfish steaks*
- *2 cloves garlic, crushed*
- *1 teaspoon finely grated fresh ginger*
- *½ teaspoon ground turmeric*
- *½ teaspoon chilli powder*
- *1 teaspoon Garam Masala (see p. 84)*
- *salt to taste*
- *lime juice*
- *oil for frying*
- *fresh coriander leaves*
- *lime wedges*

Wash fish and dry on paper towels. Mix garlic, ginger, turmeric, chilli, Garam Masala and salt with sufficient lime juice to form a paste. Rub well into both sides of fish. Cover and leave for 20 minutes.

Heat just enough oil to cover base of a large frying pan and add fish steaks. Fry over medium heat until one side is cooked, turn steaks carefully with a frying slice and fry other side. Serve garnished with coriander leaves and lime wedges.

Thai Green Curry of Fish

Serves 4

- *500 g (1 lb) jewfish, kingfish, Spanish mackerel or similar firm cutlets*
- *1½ cups canned coconut milk*
- *3 tablespoons Green Curry Paste (see Note)*
- *6 fresh, frozen or dried kaffir lime leaves*
- *½ teaspoon salt or to taste*
- *1 tablespoon fish sauce*
- *2 green chillies, seeded and chopped*
- *4 tablespoons finely chopped fresh basil leaves*

Wash fish and trim any spines with kitchen scissors. Cut into serving pieces. Mix coconut milk with an equal amount of water in a large pan. Stir in curry paste and bring to the boil, stirring constantly. Add fish, lime leaves, salt and fish sauce; reduce heat and simmer, uncovered, until fish is cooked through—about 15 minutes. Add chillies and basil and simmer a few minutes longer.

Note This delicious curry can be made in very little time if you have a home-made Green Curry Paste (see p. 83) on hand. If, however, you must use a commercial green curry paste, reduce the amount given here by half, as the commercial pastes are usually much harsher than home-made ones.

Much-prized in Singapore, this dish has its origins in India. The large pieces of flesh within the head are boneless and very sweet, and the lips and eyes are said to be the best parts.

Fish Head Curry

Serves 4

- *1 large fish head (snapper, bream) about 1.5 kg (3 lb)*
- *2 slender eggplants*
- *6 tender okra*
- *4 tablespoons peanut oil*
- *½ teaspoon fenugreek seeds*
- *1 teaspoon black mustard seeds*
- *3 green chillies, halved*
- *2 sprigs curry leaves (about 20 dried leaves)*
- *1 large onion, chopped finely*
- *2 teaspoons chopped garlic*
- *2 tablespoons ground coriander*
- *1 tablespoon ground cummin*
- *2 teaspoons ground fennel*
- *1 teaspoon ground turmeric*
- *½ teaspoon white pepper*
- *2 tablespoons tamarind pulp*
- *2 tablespoons tomato paste*
- *2 ripe tomatoes, quartered*
- *1 cup coconut milk*
- *salt to taste*

Clean and scale fish head. Cut eggplants and okra in 5 cm (2 inch) lengths. Heat oil and fry eggplant and okra for about 3 minutes, remove from oil. Add fenugreek and mustard seeds, chillies and curry leaves for 1 minute. Add onion and garlic and fry until soft and golden. Add ground spices and fry, stirring, until fragrant.

Soak tamarind pulp in 2 cups hot water for 10 minutes, squeeze to dissolve, strain. Add to pan with tomato paste and tomatoes, bring to boil, add coconut milk and salt. Add fish head and vegetables and simmer until cooked but still holding their shape. Serve with steamed white rice.

Ocean Perch with Bean Sauce

Serves 4

- *500 g (1 lb) ocean perch fillets*
- *1 teaspoon finely grated fresh ginger*
- *salt to taste*
- *1 tablespoon brown bean sauce*
- *1 tablespoon dry sherry*
- *2 tablespoons peanut oil*
- *2 thin slices ginger, shredded finely*
- *3 spring onions, shredded finely*
- *2 cloves garlic, chopped finely*

Rub fillets with grated ginger and salt and put in a heatproof dish. Cover and steam for about 5 minutes or until done. Add liquid that collects in dish to bean sauce and sherry.

Heat oil and fry ginger, spring onions and garlic for 1 minute. Stir in sauce mixture and spoon over fish.

Important in Chinese cuisine, this dish is traditionally cooked with an expensive or rare fish of delicate flavour—try large fillets of red emperor, barramundi or coral trout for example.

Steamed Red Emperor with Ham

Serves 4 to 6

- *500 g (1 lb) skinless fillets*
- *salt*
- *½ teaspoon sugar*
- *pinch white pepper*
- *1 teaspoon oriental sesame oil*
- *4 teaspoons cornflour*
- *6 dried shiitake (Chinese) mushrooms*
- *small leaves of Chinese cabbage (choysum or bok choy)*
- *125 g (4 oz) cooked ham, sliced thinly*
- *¾ cup chicken stock*

Wash fish and cut into thin slices. Sprinkle with ½ teaspoon salt, sugar, pepper, ½ teaspoon of the sesame oil and 2 teaspoons of the cornflour and mix well. Chill for 30 minutes.

Cover mushrooms with very hot water and leave to soak for 30 minutes, then cut off stems and slice caps. Trim small leaves of Chinese cabbage and take as many curved tips as there are pieces of fish. Arrange on a lightly oiled, heatproof serving dish a leaf, a slice of fish, a slice of ham cut a little smaller than the fish, and a slice of mushroom.

Steam over boiling water for 8 minutes or until fish has become opaque. While fish steams, bring chicken stock to the boil and stir in remaining 2 teaspoons cornflour mixed with a tablespoon of cold water. When sauce boils and thickens remove from heat and stir in remaining ½ teaspoon sesame oil. Season to taste with salt and white pepper. Pour over fish and serve immediately.

Goanese Fish Curry

Serves 4

- *6 large, dried red chillies*
- *500 g (1 lb) Spanish mackerel, jewfish, trevally or similar firm cutlets*
- *1 teaspoon ground turmeric*
- *salt to taste*
- *2 medium onions, chopped roughly*
- *3 cloves garlic, chopped*
- *2 teaspoons chopped fresh ginger*
- *½ cup white wine vinegar*
- *2 teaspoons ground cummin*
- *1 teaspoon shrimp paste*
- *⅓ cup oil*

Place chillies in a bowl and cover with hot water. Leave for 10 minutes. Wash and dry fish cutlets and rub surface with turmeric and salt. Drain chillies and put into blender or food processor with onions, garlic, ginger and vinegar. Process until finely ground. Mix in ground cummin and shrimp paste.

Heat oil in frying pan and fry fish pieces until golden brown on both sides. Remove from pan with spatula and set aside. Add blended mixture to oil remaining in pan and fry, stirring constantly, until dark in colour—oil will start to show around the edges. Return fish pieces to pan, spooning mixture over. Cover and simmer until fish is cooked through. Serve with rice.

Bengal Curried Fish

Serves 4

- *500 g (1 lb) ocean perch, murray cod, orange roughy or similar firm white fish steaks*
- *lemon juice*
- *2 teaspoons ground turmeric*
- *2 medium onions*
- *2 teaspoons chopped fresh ginger*
- *2 cloves garlic*
- *2 large, ripe tomatoes, chopped*
- *1 teaspoon chilli powder*
- *1 teaspoon mustard seeds*
- *¼ cup oil*
- *4 fresh green chillies, seeded and sliced*
- *salt to taste*

Wash and dry fish fillets, sprinkle with lemon juice and rub in half the turmeric. Set aside. Roughly chop one of the onions and put into a blender or food processor with ginger, garlic, tomatoes, chilli powder, mustard seeds and remaining turmeric. Blend to a purée. Cut remaining onion into fine slices.

Heat oil in a saucepan and fry sliced onion, stirring frequently, until golden. Remove onion from pan with slotted spoon and set aside. Add blended mixture and sliced chillies to oil remaining in pan. Stir over medium heat until mixture darkens in colour and oil begins to separate from mass. Add salt and 1½ cups water, then add fish cut into serving-size pieces, spooning mixture over the top. Cover and simmer for about 15 minutes, shaking pan from time to time to prevent fish from sticking. Return fried sliced onions to pan for last 5 minutes of cooking. Serve with rice.

Grilled Fish on Skewers

Serves 6

- *1 kg (2 lb) snapper, gemfish or similar thick white fillets with skin*
- *2 teaspoons finely grated fresh ginger*
- *3 cloves garlic, crushed*
- *salt to taste*
- *1 tablespoon ground coriander*
- *1 teaspoon Garam Masala (see p. 84)*
- *½ teaspoon chilli powder*
- *¼ teaspoon turmeric*
- *¼ cup lime juice*
- *1 cup plain yoghurt*
- *2 tablespoons plain flour*

Wash fish and dry on paper towel, then cut into 5 cm (2 inch) pieces. Thoroughly mix remaining ingredients in a bowl. Add fish pieces and fold gently until each piece is coated in marinade. Let stand for 15 minutes. Thread pieces of fish onto skewers—about 5 on each—making sure that skin is on one side. Put skewers on preheated grill and cook about 10 cm (4 inches) away from heat. Make sure that skin is towards heat. Grill for 4 minutes, then turn skewers and grill other side for a further 4 minutes. Do not overcook. Fish will turn opaque when ready. Serve immediately accompanied by rice and salad or fresh chutneys.

This is my family's favourite fish recipe, taught to me by my grandmother who was born and lived most of her life in Burma.

Burmese Fish Kofta Curry

Serves 6

- *1 kg (2 lb) jewfish, cod or similar white fillets*
- *1½ teaspoons salt or to taste*
- *black pepper to taste*
- *1 medium onion, chopped finely*
- *1 large clove garlic, crushed*
- *2 teaspoons finely grated fresh ginger*
- *2 tablespoons lime or lemon juice*
- *1 tablespoon finely chopped fresh dill*
- *2 slices white bread, soaked in hot water and squeezed dry*

Curry

- *2 tablespoons oriental sesame oil*
- *2 tablespoons peanut oil*
- *2 large onions, chopped finely*
- *1 tablespoon chopped garlic*
- *1 tablespoon finely chopped fresh ginger*
- *1 teaspoon ground turmeric*
- *½ teaspoon chilli powder*
- *1 teaspoon paprika, optional*
- *2 cups tomatoes, peeled and chopped*
- *salt to taste*

- *1 teaspoon dried shrimp paste*
- *2 tablespoons chopped fresh coriander leaves*
- *2 tablespoons lime or lemon juice*

Remove skin from fish with a sharp knife. Carefully remove bones and mince fish finely or chop in food processor. Place minced fish in a large bowl and thoroughly mix in remaining ingredients. Form mixture into about 24 walnut-size balls (koftas).

Curry Heat oils in a large saucepan and fry onions, garlic and ginger over gentle heat, stirring frequently, until soft and golden. Stir in turmeric, then remove from heat and add chilli powder, paprika, tomatoes and salt. Wrap dried shrimp paste in aluminium foil and cook under a hot griller for a few minutes on each side. Remove from wrapping, dissolve in 1½ cups hot water and add to pan. Cook sauce until tomato becomes soft and pulpy. Liquid must cover fish koftas, so add a little more hot water if liquid reduces too much. Gently transfer koftas to sauce and simmer over medium heat until cooked—about 20 minutes. Do not stir until koftas are cooked and firm or they will break up. Instead, shake pan gently from time to time to prevent them sticking. Stir in chopped coriander and lime or lemon juice and cook 5 minutes more. Serve with white rice and Dry Prawn Relish (see p. 74).

Variation When a more delicately flavoured dish is desired, try making fish koftas by steaming or poaching them instead of cooking them in the curry sauce. The liquid they are poached in can be thickened with a little cornflour or they can be simmered in coconut milk. Serve with steamed rice and a steamed vegetable.

Note Boneless fillets (shark sold as flake) are excellent in this dish. They can also be used to advantage in other fish curries as they are firm and do not break up when cooked.

Fish and Vermicelli Soup

Serves 6 to 8

- *500 g (1 lb) John Dory, flathead, flounder or similar white fillets*
- *2 teaspoons finely grated fresh ginger*
- *3 tablespoons fish sauce*
- *salt to taste*
- *¼ teaspoon ground black pepper*
- *60 g (2 oz) bean thread vermicelli*
- *1 tablespoon peanut oil*
- *1 medium onion, sliced thinly*
- *2 cloves garlic, crushed*
- *4 curry leaves*
- *1 teaspoon turmeric*
- *½ teaspoon dried shrimp paste*
- *2 teaspoons finely chopped lemon grass or 1 teaspoon grated lemon rind*
- *salt to taste*
- *¼ cup finely sliced spring onions*

With a sharp knife remove skin and bones from fish and coarsely chop flesh. Place in a bowl and mix with ginger, 1 tablespoon of the fish sauce, salt and pepper. Leave to marinate. Soak vermicelli in hot water to cover for 15 minutes. Heat oil in a large saucepan and gently fry onion, garlic and curry leaves, stirring frequently, until onion is soft. Add turmeric and dried shrimp paste and fry 1 minute more, crushing paste against side of pan. Add lemon grass or rind, drained vermicelli, remaining fish sauce, 6 cups hot water and salt to taste. Bring to the boil and cook for 5 minutes, then add fish, reduce heat and simmer for 5 minutes. Remove from heat, pour into serving bowl and serve sprinkled with spring onions.

Steamed Fish with Mushroom Sauce

Serves 4

- *4 dried shiitake (Chinese) mushrooms*
- *500 g (1 lb) snapper or jewfish fillets or cutlets*
- *salt and pepper to taste*
- *1 teaspoon finely grated fresh ginger*
- *sesame oil*
- *1 tablespoon peanut oil*
- *4 spring onions, chopped*
- *1 clove garlic, chopped finely*
- *1 tablespoon soy sauce*
- *1 cup fish or chicken stock*
- *1 teaspoon cornflour*
- *fresh coriander leaves*

Soak mushrooms in hot water for 30 minutes. Discard stems and cut caps into fine slices. Remove skin from fish fillets, season with salt and pepper and rub surface with ginger. Put on a plate lightly greased with sesame oil and sprinkle a little more sesame oil on top. Set aside.

Heat peanut oil in a wok and fry spring onions and garlic for a few seconds. Add mushrooms, soy sauce and stock and simmer for 10 minutes. Mix cornflour with 1 tablespoon cold water and add to wok. Stir until sauce clears and thickens. Keep warm while steaming fish. Place plate with fillets in a steamer over boiling water for about 5 minutes or until flesh becomes opaque and flakes easily. Serve with sauce poured over and sprinkled with coriander leaves.

Stir-fried Fish with Mustard Cabbage

Serves 2

- *375 g (12 oz) ling, barramundi, snapper or similar firm white fillets*
- *½ small bunch mustard cabbage (gai choy)*
- *1 tablespoon peanut oil*
- *1 spring onion, chopped finely*
- *1 small clove garlic, crushed*
- *½ teaspoon finely grated fresh ginger*
- *1 tablespoon oyster sauce*
- *1 tablespoon light soy sauce*
- *1 teaspoon cornflour*

Skin fillets and cut into bite-size pieces. Cut mustard cabbage into thick diagonal slices, separating leafy parts from stems. Heat peanut oil in a wok and fry spring onion over gentle heat just until soft. Add garlic and ginger and stir for a few seconds, then increase heat to medium and toss in mustard cabbage stems. Stir-fry for 1 minute, then add oyster and soy sauces with ¼ cup hot water. Cover and simmer for 1 minute.

Add fish pieces and leafy parts of mustard cabbage and stir gently just until fish becomes opaque. Mix cornflour with 1 tablespoon cold water and stir into liquid. Bring mixture to the boil, stirring until it thickens slightly. Serve immediately.

Variations on this method of 'cooking' fish abound throughout the Pacific. The acid in lime or lemon juice turns the flesh opaque the same way that heat does. Choose a delicately flavoured fish.

Marinated Fish Salad

Serves 4

- *500 g (1 lb) white fish fillets*
- *lime or lemon juice*
- *salt to taste*
- *1 purple onion, sliced very thinly*
- *1 large, green capsicum, diced*
- *3 spring onions, sliced finely*
- *2 firm, red tomatoes, peeled and diced*
- *1 cup canned coconut milk*
- *1 small clove garlic, crushed*
- *½ teaspoon finely grated fresh ginger*
- *salt and ground black pepper to taste*
- *⅛ teaspoon ground turmeric*
- *lettuce leaves, washed*
- *chopped coriander leaves*

Remove skin and any bones from fillets. Cut fish into bite-size pieces and put into a glass or ceramic bowl. Add sufficient strained lime juice to cover. Stir in salt and onion with a wooden spoon. (Do not use metal utensils.) Cover and refrigerate for at least 8 hours, stirring once or twice during marination. Chill prepared vegetables.

Mix coconut milk, garlic, ginger, salt, pepper and turmeric. Drain excess lime juice from fish. Add coconut dressing and mix well. Add prepared vegetables, except for lettuce. Toss and serve on a dish lined with lettuce leaves. Garnish with coriander leaves.

Thai Fish with Coconut Milk

Serves 4

- *500 g (1 lb) sea perch, ling or salmon fillets*
- *2 large dried chillies*
- *2 large cloves garlic*
- *2 kaffir lime leaves*
- *1 slice galangal*
- *2 stalks lemon grass, sliced finely*
- *2 cups canned coconut milk*
- *2 tablespoons fish sauce*
- *oil for frying*
- *5 small dried chillies*
- *2 tablespoons chopped roasted peanuts*
- *fresh basil sprigs*

Remove any bones from fish and cut fillets into serving pieces. Discard stalks and seeds from large chillies; soak in hot water for 10 minutes. Drain and put into a blender with garlic, lime leaves, galangal and lemon grass, adding a little coconut milk, and blend to a paste.

Heat 1 cup of coconut milk in a wok over gentle heat until oil begins to float on top—about 10 minutes. Add blended mixture and fry, stirring constantly, until it smells cooked and fragrant.

Add fish pieces, turning to coat in mixture, then add remaining coconut milk and fish sauce with 1 cup water. Stir to mix and simmer just until fish is cooked. Heat oil in a small frying pan and fry small chillies for a few seconds. Set aside. Add peanuts to fish just before end of cooking time and serve garnished with fried chillies and basil.

Fish Fillets in Hoi Sin Sauce

Serves 3 to 4

- *375 g (12 oz) bream, John Dory, snapper or similar fresh white fish fillets*
- *2 tablespoons peanut oil*
- *1 large clove garlic, bruised*
- *1 tablespoon light soy sauce*
- *1 teaspoon finely grated fresh ginger*
- *1 teaspoon hoi sin sauce*
- *shreds of spring onion for garnish*

With a sharp knife remove skin from fish. Rinse fillets and dry on paper towels. Heat oil in a wok and fry garlic until golden, then remove and discard. Put fillets into oil one at a time; turn each after a few seconds and move to side of wok before adding the next. When all fish has been fried, sprinkle with soy sauce and ginger, cover and simmer for 1 minute. Remove wok from heat and stir hoi sin sauce into liquid. Arrange fish on platter, spoon sauce over and garnish with spring onion shreds. Serve with steamed rice.

Marinated Bonito

Serves 4

- *500 g (1 lb) bonito fillets*
- *sea salt*
- *½ cup rice vinegar*
- *2 tablespoons sugar*
- *¼ cup each shredded white radish and carrot*
- *watercress sprigs*
- *wasabi*

Dipping Sauce

- *1 teaspoon grated fresh ginger*
- *3 tablespoons Japanese soy sauce*
- *2 tablespoons rice vinegar*
- *1 tablespoon mirin or sweet sherry*
- *1 tablespoon sugar*

Rub bonito fillets liberally with salt and refrigerate overnight. Rinse off excess salt, cut into thin slices and marinate for 30 minutes in a mixture of vinegar, sugar and 2 tablespoons cold water. Arrange on individual plates and garnish with radish, carrot and watercress. Add a small cone of wasabi.

Dipping Sauce Stir ingredients until sugar dissolves. Serve in individual bowls.

Otak Otak is probably best described as an exotic and unusually flavoursome fish cake traditionally cooked in banana or coconut leaves (see Note).

Otak Otak

Serves 4

- *500 g (1 lb) white fish fillets*
- *3 dried red chillies*
- *2 stems lemon grass, sliced finely or 2 strips lemon rind*
- *1 medium onion, peeled and chopped roughly*
- *1 teaspoon chopped garlic*
- *½ teaspoon ground turmeric*
- *1 teaspoon salt*
- *¼ teaspoon pepper*
- *2 teaspoons ground coriander*
- *3 tablespoons thick coconut milk*
- *4 candlenuts or macadamia nuts, optional*

⅓ cup chopped Vietnamese mint or fresh coriander

- *2 fresh red chillies, chopped finely*

Remove any skin and bones from fillets and purée in a food processor. Discard stems and seeds of chillies and soak in hot water for 10 minutes. Put chillies, lemon grass, onion, garlic, turmeric, salt, pepper, coriander, coconut milk and nuts into a blender or food processor and blend to a purée. Mix well with fish, adding mint and chillies.

Put a tablespoon of mixture onto a square of banana leaf or onto a square of heavy-duty foil. Shape into flat parcels, fold foil over to seal edges and cook over a barbecue or under a preheated grill for 5 minutes each side. Serve warm or cold as an appetiser.

Note If using banana leaves, first wash, dry and heat over low flame to make them pliable before making the parcels. Fasten with toothpicks.

Molluscs and Bivalves

Under this heading come abalone, scallops, oysters, pipis and other species with a soft body within two shells. Ensure the shells are firmly closed, or closed when handled (this means that the creature is alive). Keep them cool and damp but do not refrigerate them as the cold will kill them. When heated, they pop open and are cooked (some take longer to cook than others, but discard any that refuse to open).

Scallops with Snow Peas

Serves 4

- *375 g (12 oz) fresh scallops*
- *125 g (4 oz) snow peas*
- *2 tablespoons peanut oil*
- *½ teaspoon finely grated fresh ginger*
- *2 large cloves garlic, chopped finely*
- *4 spring onions, chopped*
- *1 tablespoon light soy sauce*
- *1 tablespoon dry sherry*
- *1 teaspoon oriental sesame oil*

Remove any dark streaks from scallops. String snow peas and slice diagonally into halves if large. Heat peanut oil in a wok and stir-fry ginger, garlic and spring onions over low heat until soft, but not browned. Increase heat, toss in snow peas and stir-fry for 1 minute. Add scallops and stir-fry 1 minute more. Stir in soy sauce and sherry. Cover and simmer for 2 minutes, then sprinkle with sesame oil and mix. Serve immediately with rice.

A savoury Japanese custard dish served cold in summer and eaten with a spoon.

Steamed Egg Custard with Shellfish

Serves 4

- *4 dried shiitake (Chinese) mushrooms*
- *2 tablespoons Japanese soy sauce*
- *1 tablespoon sugar*
- *2 large spinach leaves*
- *4 fresh scallops*
- *4 fresh oysters*
- *fresh mustard sprigs and cress sprouts*

Custard

- *4 eggs*
- *2½ cups dashi stock (see Note)*
- *salt to taste*
- *1 tablespoon Japanese soy sauce*
- *2 tablespoons sake, mirin or dry sherry*

Soak mushrooms in hot water for 30 minutes. Discard stems and simmer caps in ½ cup soaking water with soy sauce and sugar for 8 to 10 minutes. Cut in halves. Wash spinach leaves, blanch briefly with boiling water, then drain on paper towel. Cut into large pieces, discarding stems.

In individual custard cups or ramekins place a mushroom, a scallop, an oyster and some spinach. Fill cups with custard mixture, carefully skimming off bubbles from top of mixture. Place cups in a baking pan with hot water to come halfway up the sides. Bake in moderate oven, 180°C (350°F), for 15 minutes or until set. Serve warm, garnished with a tiny bunch of mustard and cress sprouts or a sprig of watercress.

Custard Beat eggs, then stir in remaining ingredients.

Note Make up dashi stock following instructions on packet or bottle of dashi concentrate.

A Japanese dish served in small, deep bowls as an appetiser or side salad.

Abalone with Vinegar and Sesame

Serves 6 to 8

- *1 can Japanese abalone*
- *2 small seedless green cucumbers*
- *salt to taste*

Dressing

- *2 tablespoons sesame seeds*
- *½ teaspoon finely grated fresh ginger*
- *1 tablespoon sugar*
- *¼ cup rice vinegar or mild white wine vinegar*
- *1 sheet nori (dried seaweed)*

Drain abalone and cut into paper-thin slices. Cut cucumbers in halves lengthwise. Cut across into thin slices. Place in a colander, sprinkling with a little salt and leave to drain for 20 minutes. Rinse briefly with cold water. Leave to drain well.

Dressing Toast sesame seeds in a dry pan over medium heat, stirring constantly, until golden—this should only take a few minutes. Turn out to cool, then crush slightly with a mortar and pestle or in a blender. Mix with ginger, sugar, vinegar and 2 tablespoons water. Lightly toast nori until crisp, and cut into thin strips with kitchen scissors.

Mix abalone and cucumber slices; pour Dressing over and chill. Serve sprinkled with shredded nori.

Abalone in Oyster Sauce

Serves 4

- *4 dried shiitake (Chinese) mushrooms*
- *1 x 450 g (1 lb) can abalone*
- *24 snow peas*
- *4 spring onions*

Sauce

- *1 tablespoon oyster sauce*
- *2 teaspoons light soy sauce*
- *1 tablespoon dry sherry*
- *2 teaspoons cornflour*

Place mushrooms in a small bowl and soak in hot water for 30 minutes, then discard stalks and cut each mushroom into halves or quarters. Drain abalone, reserving liquid. Cut abalone into paper-thin slices. Remove strings from snow peas. Cut spring onion on the diagonal into bite-size pieces.

Sauce In a bowl mix oyster sauce, soy sauce and dry sherry. Gradually add cornflour, mixing until smooth. Stir in liquid from can. Pour into a saucepan and bring to the boil, stirring constantly. Add mushrooms, snow peas and spring onions. Cook, stirring constantly, until vegetables are tender but still crisp—about 2 minutes. Add abalone and just heat through. Be careful not to cook it on high heat as it will become tough. Serve with steamed rice.

As scallops are expensive, use a smaller amount and add a delicately flavoured vegetable.

Stir-fried Scallops

Serves 2

- *250 g (8 oz) fresh scallops*
- *2 choy sum (Chinese cabbage) or 3 stems celery*
- *2 tablespoons peanut oil*
- *1 teaspoon finely grated fresh ginger*
- *4 spring onions, sliced finely*
- *1 tablespoon dry sherry*
- *2 teaspoons light soy sauce*

Remove any dark streaks from scallops. Cut choy sum or celery into thin diagonal slices. Heat oil in wok and fry ginger over medium heat for 1 minute.

Add scallops and stir-fry on medium heat just until opaque—about 1 minute. Add choy sum or celery and spring onions and toss for 1 minute more. Stir in sherry and soy sauce until well mixed. Serve immediately with plain white rice.

Spicy Coconut Mussels

Serves 4

- *1 kg (2 lb) fresh mussels (see Note)*
- *3 tablespoons ghee or oil*
- *2 medium onions, chopped finely*
- *4 cloves garlic, chopped finely*
- *2 teaspoons finely chopped fresh ginger*
- *3 fresh red chillies, seeded and chopped*
- *½ teaspoon ground turmeric*
- *1 tablespoon ground coriander*
- *salt to taste*
- *lime juice to taste*
- *1 cup grated fresh coconut or ½ cup desiccated coconut (see Note)*
- *1 tablespoon chopped fresh coriander leaves*

Scrub mussels thoroughly under cold, running water and remove beards. Discard mussels that are not tightly closed. Heat ghee in a large, deep saucepan and fry onions, garlic and ginger over medium heat, stirring frequently, until onions are soft and golden. Add chillies, turmeric and ground coriander and cook, stirring, for 3 minutes. Stir in salt and 1 cup water, bring to the boil and simmer, covered, for 5 minutes. Add mussels, cover and steam for a few minutes, transferring those that have opened to a serving dish. Continue cooking remainder and discard any that refuse to open. Stir lime juice into sauce remaining in pan. Spoon sauce over mussels, sprinkle with coconut and coriander leaves and serve immediately with steamed white rice.

Note The instructions given here are for live black mussels. Remember that mussels which are not tightly closed before cooking or do not open after cooking should be discarded. You can also use cooked mussels in this dish and simply make the spicy sauce and stir in the mussels until heated.

If using desiccated coconut, moisten it with a little water.

Mussels or Clams in Red Curry Sauce

Serves 4

- *1 kg (2 lb) fresh mussels or clams*
- *¾ cup canned coconut milk*
- *2 tablespoons Red Curry Paste (see p. 83)*
- *2 kaffir lime leaves*
- *1–2 tablespoons fish sauce*
- *1 teaspoon brown sugar or palm sugar*
- *2 tablespoons lime juice*
- *1 red chilli, sliced finely*
- *2 spring onions, sliced diagonally*

Scrub mussels under cold water, removing beards. Discard those with open shells. If using clams, rinse. Place in a large saucepan and add ¾ cup water. Cover and cook over high heat, shaking pan occasionally. Shells should open after a few minutes. Remove and discard top shells and any that remain closed. Strain cooking liquid through a fine sieve.

Heat ½ cup of the coconut milk in a saucepan until oil appears around edges, mix in Red Curry Paste and cook, stirring, until fragrant. Stir in remaining coconut milk, the reserved cooking liquid, lime leaves, fish sauce and sugar and stir until mixture simmers. Simmer for 10 minutes, stirring frequently. Add lime juice, red chilli and spring onions, ladle over mussels or clams. Serve with rice.

Octopus and Squid

Squid Sambal

Serves 4 to 6

- *500 g (1 lb) small squid*
- *2 onions, chopped roughly*
- *3 cloves garlic*
- *½ teaspoon dried shrimp paste*
- *1 stalk fresh lemon grass, sliced finely*
- *3 teaspoons sambal ulek*
- *1 teaspoon dried tamarind*
- *3 tablespoons peanut oil*
- *2 teaspoons brown sugar*
- *1 teaspoon paprika*

Clean squid, removing and discarding head and ink sac. Cut off and reserve tentacles. Clean out body cavity, washing thoroughly. Rub spotted skin from squid. Slice body across into rings. Put onions, garlic, shrimp paste, lemon grass and sambal ulek into a blender or food processor and blend until smooth, scraping down sides of container and adding a little water if necessary.

Heat oil in a wok and add blended mixture. Cook, stirring, over medium heat until it is a dark colour and oil appears around edges. Dissolve tamarind in ½ cup hot water, strain and discard seeds. Add to wok with sugar and paprika. Stir in squid. Cook uncovered, stirring until gravy is thick and oily and squid is tender, adding water if necessary. Serve as an accompaniment with rice.

Squid with Pork Stuffing

Serves 6 to 8

- *6 dried shiitake (Chinese) mushrooms*
- *10 dried lily flowers (Golden Needles)*
- *½ cup bean thread vermicelli*
- *250 g (8 oz) minced pork*
- *2 cloves garlic, crushed*
- *1 teaspoon grated fresh ginger*
- *3 spring onions, chopped finely*
- *salt to taste*
- *1 tablespoon fish sauce*
- *¼ teaspoon ground black pepper*
- *500 g (1 lb) fresh squid*
- *peanut oil for frying*
- *shredded lettuce*

Soak mushrooms and lily flowers in hot water for 30 minutes. In a separate bowl soak vermicelli in hot water for 20 minutes. Discard mushroom stems and any tough parts of the flowers. Finely chop remainder, place in a bowl and mix with pork. Drain and chop vermicelli and add to pork. Add garlic, ginger, spring onions, salt, fish sauce and pepper to pork mixture and combine until well mixed.

Clean squid thoroughly, discarding head, 'beak' and contents of body. Reserve tentacles, chop finely and add to pork mixture. Wash squid inside and out with cold, running water, rubbing off spotted skin. Pack pork mixture into squid and sew opening shut with a coarse needle and thread or fasten with wooden cocktail sticks.

Heat about ¼ cup oil in a wok or frying pan and sauté squid over medium heat for 5 minutes. Prick surface of each squid with a fine skewer and continue frying for a further 10 minutes (or longer if squid is large). When cooked and half cool, cut into slices and arrange on shredded lettuce.

Squid Curry

Serves 4

- *500 g (1 lb) fresh squid*
- *1 medium onion, chopped finely*
- *2 cloves garlic, crushed*
- *1 teaspoon finely grated fresh ginger*
- *salt to taste*
- *1 teaspoon chilli powder*
- *½ teaspoon dried shrimp paste*
- *1 cup canned coconut milk*
- *8 candlenuts or 4 brazil nuts, grated*
- *1 stalk fresh lemon grass, sliced finely*
- *1 teaspoon brown sugar*
- *1 teaspoon tamarind concentrate*

Clean squid, removing and discarding head and ink sac. Cut off tentacles and reserve. Wash squid thoroughly inside and out, then rub spotted skin from body. Slice squid lengthwise into halves. Cut into bite-size pieces. Put remaining ingredients, except sugar and tamarind, into a saucepan. Add 1 cup water and bring to a simmer, stirring constantly. Simmer mixture, uncovered, until thickened, stirring occasionally. Meanwhile dissolve sugar and tamarind in ¼ cup hot water. Add squid pieces and tentacles to saucepan and simmer for only a few minutes—any longer will toughen the squid. Stir in sugar and tamarind mixture, adding more salt to taste as required. Serve hot with rice and vegetables.

For a decorative effect, large squid tubes with thick walls are best as the flesh is easier to score.

Szechwan-style Squid

Serves 6

- *500 g (1 lb) squid tubes*
- *½ teaspoon salt*
- *1 egg white*
- *1 tablespoon peanut oil*
- *2 tablespoons cornflour*
- *1 red capsicum*
- *4 spring onions*
- *3 cups peanut oil for deep-frying*
- *1 teaspoon finely chopped garlic*
- *1 teaspoon finely chopped ginger*
- *1 tablespoon bottled hot radish*
- *½ cup chicken stock*
- *½ teaspoon oriental sesame oil*
- *chilli flowers for garnish*

Cut tubes open lengthways and if necessary rinse off sand. With a sharp knife score inside surface diagonally, holding knife at a 45° angle and making parallel lines 6 mm (¼ inch) apart. Then make lines at right angles to the first ones. Divide into bite-size pieces about 5 cm (2 inches) square.

Season squid with salt and pour over it slightly beaten egg white, oil and 1½ tablespoons of the cornflour. Mix well, cover and chill for 30 minutes or more.

Cut capsicum and spring onions into bite-size strips and set aside.

Heat 3 cups peanut oil in a wok and when medium hot drop in squid, stirring to keep pieces separate. They will curl and become white in 1 minute or less. Immediately lift out on a wire spoon and drain. Pour off oil and return wok to heat with just the film of oil that remains. Stir-fry garlic, ginger, capsicum and spring onions for 1 minute, add hot radish and toss, then add stock and bring to the boil. Thicken with remaining cornflour mixed with 2 tablespoons cold water. Stir in squid and sesame oil, toss well and serve at once, garnished with chilli flowers.

Stir-fried Squid with Capsicums

Serves 4

- *500 g (1 lb) large squid tubes*
- *1 red and 1 green capsicum*
- *3 tablespoons peanut oil*
- *1 teaspoon finely grated fresh ginger*
- *1 clove garlic, crushed*
- *4 spring onions, sliced diagonally*
- *1 teaspoon sugar*
- *1 tablespoon light soy sauce*
- *1 tablespoon dry sherry*
- *2 teaspoons chilli sauce*
- *1 teaspoon cornflour*

Slit squid tubes lengthwise and lightly score inner surface, making a criss-cross pattern. Cut into pieces about 5 cm x 2.5 cm (2 inches x 1 inch). Cut capsicums into bite-size pieces.

Heat oil in wok, and stir-fry squid over high heat just until it curls—about 1 minute. Remove with slotted spoon and drain on paper towel. Stir-fry ginger, garlic, capsicum and spring onions for 1 minute, then add sugar, soy sauce, sherry and chilli sauce. Mix cornflour with 1 tablespoon water, add to wok and stir until mixture thickens. Mix squid into sauce. Serve with steamed rice.

FRIED SQUID CURRY

Serves 6

- *1 kg (2 lb) squid*
- *2 medium onions, chopped finely*
- *4 cloves garlic, chopped finely*
- *2 teaspoons finely grated fresh ginger*
- *1 teaspoon ground turmeric*
- *2 tablespoons Ceylon Curry Powder* *(see p. 84)*
- *½ teaspoon whole cummin seeds*
- *1 small stick cinnamon*
- *1 stalk fresh lemon grass*
- *8 curry leaves*
- *3 tablespoons vinegar*
- *1½ cups canned coconut milk*
- *1½ teaspoons salt, or to taste*
- *2 teaspoons peanut oil for frying*

Clean squid, discarding head and ink sac. Cut off and reserve tentacles. Rub spotted skin from body and wash inside and out. Slice body across into rings. Put into a large saucepan with tentacles and all ingredients except oil. Add 1½ cups water, stir and bring to the boil. Reduce heat and simmer for 1 hour, or until squid is tender and sauce has thickened. Remove squid pieces from sauce with a slotted spoon and fry in oil. Pour sauce into pan in which squid was fried. Simmer for 2 minutes. Serve with white rice and accompaniments.

Octopus is generally tougher than squid, but it is possible to purchase it already tenderised at fish markets or retail outlets.

Octopus Salad

Serves 4

- *500 g (1 lb) tiny octopus if available*
- *3 kaffir lime leaves*
- *2 sprigs coriander, including roots*
- *1 stalk lemon grass, sliced*
- *1 tablespoon fish sauce*
- *2 tablespoons lime juice*
- *2 teaspoons brown sugar*
- *2 small cloves garlic, crushed*
- *1 teaspoon finely grated fresh ginger*
- *½ teaspoon black pepper*
- *½ cup finely sliced spring onions, cut on diagonal*
- *¼ cup fresh mint leaves*
- *¼ cup fresh coriander leaves*
- *2 fresh red chillies, sliced finely*
- *lettuce leaves*

With a sharp knife cut through flesh of octopus below eyes and discard head. Pick up body section with tentacles attached, push out beak and discard. Can be left whole or larger ones cut into pieces. Wash well and drain. Bring 3 cups water to the boil in a small saucepan with kaffir lime leaves, coriander sprigs and lemon grass. Let boil for 5 minutes. Drop in octopus and as soon as it turns opaque remove with a slotted spoon. This should take no more than 1 minute. If octopus is large, allow more time.

In a bowl mix fish sauce, lime juice, brown sugar, garlic, ginger and black pepper. Add cooked octopus and toss until well coated in dressing. Gently mix in spring onions, mint, coriander and chillies. Serve on lettuce leaves.

Barbecued Octopus

Serves 4 to 6

- *1 kg (2 lb) small octopus*
- *1 small clove garlic, crushed*
- *1 teaspoon sugar*
- *1 teaspoon finely grated fresh ginger*
- *6 tablespoons Japanese soy sauce*
- *6 tablespoons rice wine (mirin)*
- *vegetable oil for cooking*
- *lettuce and watercress*

Clean octopus by slitting open head and removing gut and beak and cutting out eyes. Wash well and drain. You can leave tiny octopus whole or cut into pieces. Crush garlic with sugar and mix in a bowl with ginger, soy sauce and mirin. Put octopus in bowl and toss with marinade until all pieces are coated. Leave for 30 minutes. Remove octopus from bowl, allowing excess marinade to drain back, and grill over glowing coals or on hot griddle plate, turning frequently, just until flesh is uniformly opaque. Be careful not to overcook as this toughens octopus.

Add ¼ cup water to remaining marinade and quickly bring to the boil in a small saucepan. Serve octopus with sauce spooned over and accompanied by lettuce and watercress.

Mixed Seafood Dishes

A combination of different seafood is popular in many Asian cultures. Even combinations of seafood and pork or bacon to enhance the flavour are a tasty alternative.

Basic Fish or Prawn Stock

- *fish heads and trimmings or prawn heads and shells*
- *¼ teaspoon black peppercorns*
- *3 slices fresh ginger*
- *1 carrot, halved*
- *2 stalks celery with leaves*
- *1 large onion*
- *2 stalks fresh coriander*

Wash fish pieces or prawn heads and shells thoroughly. Put into a large saucepan with cold water to cover. Add remaining ingredients and bring to the boil. Cover and simmer for 20 minutes if using fish, 40 minutes if using prawns. Strain stock and use in soups or other seafood recipes.

Fish with Crab Sauce

Serves 4

- *750 g (1½ lb) silver dory, John Dory or similar white fillets*
- *1 teaspoon finely grated fresh ginger*
- *salt to taste*
- *2 tablespoons cornflour*
- *oil for deep-frying*

Crab Sauce

- *2 tablespoons peanut oil*
- *6 spring onions, chopped*
- *½ teaspoon finely grated fresh ginger*
- *½ cup chicken stock*
- *185 g (6 oz) crabmeat (see Note)*
- *¼ teaspoon white pepper*
- *2 teaspoons cornflour*
- *salt to taste*

Remove skin from fish using a sharp knife. Wash fillets and dry with paper towel. Place fillets on chopping board and rub with grated ginger. Cut in halves lengthwise and then into bite-size pieces. Toss in a mixture of salt and cornflour.

Heat oil in a wok or small, deep frying pan and fry fish, several pieces at a time, over medium heat for about 1 minute. As each batch is cooked, drain on paper towel and keep warm while making sauce.

Crab Sauce Heat oil in a pan and fry spring onions and ginger over low heat for a few seconds, stirring constantly. Add stock, cover and simmer for a few minutes. Stir in crabmeat and season to taste with pepper. Mix cornflour with 1 tablespoon cold water until smooth, stir into sauce and season to taste with salt if necessary. Arrange fish pieces on dish, spoon sauce over and serve immediately.

Note It is now possible to buy packets of fresh crabmeat—a great improvement on the rather dry texture of canned crab. Ask your fish supplier.

Grilled Mixed Seafood

Serves 4

- *1 small clove garlic*
- *1 teaspoon sugar*
- *½ teaspoon finely grated fresh ginger*
- *3 tablespoons Japanese soy sauce*
- *4 small ling or snapper fillets or steaks*
- *8 large raw prawns*
- *8 fresh oysters*
- *8 fresh scallops*
- *1 large green capsicum*
- *1 small eggplant*
- *vegetable oil for cooking*

Dipping Sauce

- *½ cup Japanese soy sauce*
- *¼ cup rice wine (mirin)*
- *3 teaspoons sugar*
- *1 teaspoon finely grated fresh ginger*
- *1 teaspoon oriental sesame oil*

Crush garlic with sugar and mix with ginger and soy sauce in a bowl. Add fish fillets, turning until they are coated in marinade. Set aside for 30 minutes. Meanwhile shell and devein prawns, leaving tail intact. Drain any liquid from oysters. Remove any dark streaks from scallops, rinse briefly and drain. Cut capsicum lengthwise into eighths, discarding seeds and membranes. Slice eggplant across into rounds.

Heat barbecue hotplate or griddle and grease lightly. Start with capsicum and eggplant as they take longer to cook, then add fish fillets, prawns, oysters and scallops as required and cook just until done. Turn pieces over to ensure even cooking and be careful not to overcook as this will make the seafood dry and tough. Oysters and scallops need a very short cooking time—just enough to heat them through. Serve with Dipping Sauce and hot white rice.

Dipping Sauce Mix soy sauce, rice wine, sugar, ginger and sesame oil, stirring until sugar is dissolved. Divide among individual sauce bowls.

Stuffed Fried Crab

Serves 4

- *4 cooked blue swimmer crabs*
- *250 g (8 oz) raw prawns, shelled and deveined*
- *½ cup boiled bean thread vermicelli*
- *125 g (4 oz) minced pork*
- *2 tablespoons finely chopped spring onions*
- *2 cloves garlic, crushed*
- *salt to taste*
- *ground black pepper to taste*
- *2 tablespoons chopped coriander leaves*
- *1 teaspoon finely chopped red chilli*
- *1 tablespoon cornflour*
- *1 egg, beaten*
- *peanut oil for frying*
- *coriander sprigs or chilli flowers*

Carefully remove top shell from crabs, scrub away any patches and dry shells. Discard grey, feathery gills and stomach bag. Crack open bodies and claws, remove meat and set aside. Chop prawns finely. Cut vermicelli into 2.5 cm (1 inch) lengths. Put crab meat, prawns, vermicelli, pork and spring onions into a bowl.

Mix garlic, salt, pepper, coriander and chilli into beaten egg. Add to ingredients in bowl and mix thoroughly. Fill crab shells with mixture. Heat at least 3 cups oil in a wok or deep frying pan and fry crabs, ladling oil over top. Continue frying over medium heat for about 7 or 8 minutes so that by the time mixture is golden brown on top, it is cooked through. Drain on paper towel, arrange on serving plate and garnish with sprigs of coriander and chilli flowers if desired.

Braised Fish and Prawn Rolls

Serves 4 to 6

- *12 raw prawns, shelled and deveined*
- *½ teaspoon finely grated fresh ginger*
- *1 small clove garlic, crushed*
- *1 tablespoon finely chopped coriander leaves*
- *500 g (1 lb) John Dory or similar flat, firm white fillets*
- *2 tablespoons peanut oil*
- *1 tablespoon light soy sauce*
- *1 tablespoon dry sherry*
- *3 spring onions, sliced finely*

Finely chop prawns and combine with ginger, garlic and coriander leaves. Remove skin and bones from fish fillets. Cut into 12 strips large enough to roll round a portion of prawn. Fasten with wooden toothpicks.

Heat peanut oil in a wok; add fish rolls and fry for 2 minutes, turning carefully with chopsticks or tongs. Stir in ¼ cup hot water with soy sauce and sherry. Cover and simmer gently for a few minutes until fish becomes evenly opaque. Remove rolls to a serving dish with slotted spoon. Add spring onions to wok and stir, then pour sauce over fish rolls. Serve immediately.

The fine translucent noodles that form a crisp coating around the seafood when deep-fried are known in Japan as harusame *which translates as 'spring rain'.*

Deep-fried Seafood with Noodles
Harusame Tempura

Serves 4

- *500 g (1 lb) fillets firm white fish*
- *12 medium-size raw prawns*
- *1 tablespoon Japanese soy sauce*
- *1 tablespoon rice wine (mirin)*
- *salt to taste*
- *harusame or bean thread noodles*
- *½ cup cornflour*
- *1 to 2 egg whites, beaten until frothy*
- *vegetable oil for deep frying*

Tempura Sauce

- *3 tablespoons rice wine (mirin)*
- *3 tablespoons Japanese soy sauce*
- *1 cup dashi (see Note)*
- *salt to taste*

Remove skin and any bones from fillets. Cut fish into bite-size lengths. Shell and devein prawns, leaving tails intact. Marinate seafood in mixture of soy sauce, rice wine and salt for 30 minutes. Using kitchen scissors cut noodles, a few strands at a time, into 12 mm (½ inch) lengths. You will need about 1½ cups. Roll each piece of seafood first in cornflour, dusting off excess, then in egg white and last in noodles.

Heat oil until hot and drop in seafood a few pieces at a time. The noodles should puff immediately; if they do not it means that the oil is not hot enough and the harusame will be tough and leathery instead of light and crisp. Fry for no more than 1 minute and remove from oil with wire strainer before colour changes. Drain on paper towel and serve with Tempura Sauce.

Tempura Sauce Heat rice wine in a small saucepan, then remove from heat and ignite with a match. Shake pan gently until flame dies, add remaining ingredients and bring quickly to the boil. Cool to room temperature. Adjust seasoning if necessary.

Snapper with Black Beans

Serves 4

- *4 medium-size snapper cutlets or fillets*
- *salt to taste*
- *1 teaspoon grated ginger*
- *1 small clove garlic, crushed*
- *2 spring onions, sliced diagonally*
- *2 teaspoons canned, salted black beans, rinsed*
- *1 tablespoon light soy sauce*
- *1 tablespoon dry sherry*
- *2 rashers bacon, chopped*

Rub cutlets with salt, ginger and garlic. Place on an oiled heatproof plate, sprinkle with spring onions, black beans, soy and sherry. Steam until fish is opaque. Fry bacon until crisp, srpinkle over fish and serve immediately.

Fish and Prawn Layers

Serves 6

- *500 g (1 lb) bream, snapper or similar firm white fish fillets*
- *250 g (8 oz) raw prawns, shelled and deveined*
- *1 small clove garlic, crushed*
- *½ teaspoon finely grated fresh ginger*
- *½ cup finely chopped spring onions*
- *2 tablespoons finely chopped water chestnuts*
- *salt to taste*
- *1 teaspoon cornflour*
- *1 teaspoon sesame oil*

Sauce

- *1 tablespoon peanut oil*
- *125 g (4 oz) snow peas, strings removed*
- *1 tablespoon oyster sauce*
- *1 cup chicken stock*
- *1 tablespoon dry sherry*
- *1 teaspoon rice vinegar*
- *½ teaspoon sugar*
- *3 teaspoons cornflour*

With a sharp knife remove skin and any small bones from fish fillets. Chop prawns finely and place in a bowl with garlic, ginger, half the spring onions, water chestnuts, salt, cornflour and sesame oil. Combine until thoroughly mixed. Spread mixture over surface of fillets with a spatula and then cut fillets into 12 pieces of equal size. Lightly grease a large plate with sesame oil and place fish on it. Place plate in steamer over boiling water and steam until fish becomes opaque. Remove from heat and keep warm.

Sauce Heat peanut oil in wok, add remaining spring onions and stir-fry for 10 seconds. Add snow peas and stir-fry 1 minute. Add oyster sauce, stock, sherry, vinegar and sugar, bring to the boil. Mix cornflour with 1 tablespoon cold water and stir into sauce until it boils and thickens. Remove from heat. Arrange snow peas on plate with fish, then spoon remaining sauce over. Serve immediately.

Dried Seafoods

The harvest of the sea is an important source of protein to the large population of Asia. When not eaten fresh, it is dried, salted or fermented. In some instances it is used as a flavouring—a mere teaspoonful can bring great flavour to a dish; in others dried or salted fish is the main ingredient.

Dry Prawn Relish
Balachaung

Makes about 4 cups

- *20 cloves garlic*
- *2 cups peanut oil*
- *4 medium onions, sliced finely*
- *1 x 250 g (8 oz) packet dried prawn powder*
- *2 teaspoons chilli powder*
- *2 teaspoons salt*
- *1 teaspoon dried shrimp paste (ngapi)*
- *½ cup vinegar*

Peel garlic, cut into thin slices. Heat oil and fry onion and garlic separately over low heat until golden. Lift out with frying spatula and set aside on paper towel. They will become crisp and darken as they cool.

Pour off oil and reserve, leaving about 1 cup in pan. Add prawn powder and fry over low heat for 5 minutes. All prawn powder should be moistened by oil—if there is insufficient, add a little more reserved oil. Add chilli powder, salt and shrimp paste mixed with vinegar. Stir well and fry until crisp. Cool completely, then stir in fried onion and garlic until well mixed. Bottle in an airtight jar. Keeps well.

A quickly made accompaniment to Thai curry and rice.

Dried Shrimp Salad

Serves 4

- *¼ cup dried shrimps*
- *1 stalk lemon grass*
- *2 shallots, peeled and sliced*
- *3 fresh red chillies*
- *1 tablespoon sugar*
- *¼ cup fresh lime juice*
- *1 tablespoon fish sauce*

Put dried shrimp in a bowl and cover with hot water. Set aside to soak for 10 minutes or until shrimps are soft, then drain. Remove any dark veins. Finely slice only tender white and pale green part of lemon grass. Slice chillies in half lengthwise and carefully remove seeds with point of a knife. Cut chillies into fine slices. In a serving bowl mix sugar, lime juice and fish sauce. Add all prepared ingredients and toss until mixed. Serve garnished with chilli flower.

A dip for crisp crackers or an accompaniment to rice.

Shrimp and Tamarind Dip

Makes about 2 cups

- *8 large dried chillies*
- *1 cup dried shrimps*
- *2 medium onions, chopped roughly*
- *6 cloves garlic*
- *½ cup peanut oil*
- *1 tablespoon tamarind pulp*
- *½ cup brown sugar*
- *2 tablespoons fish sauce*
- *1 tablespoon lime juice*

Break ends from chillies; shake out seeds and discard. Place chillies in a bowl, cover with boiling water and let soak for 15 minutes. Put dried shrimps into a blender and blend until reduced to a floss. Transfer to a bowl and put drained chillies, onions, garlic and a little water into blender and blend to a purée.

Heat peanut oil in a frying pan and fry purée over medium heat, stirring constantly, until oil separates. Dissolve tamarind in ½ cup water and stir into pan with sugar and shrimp floss. Simmer for 5 minutes more or until a thick dipping consistency. Add fish sauce and simmer for 2 to 3 minutes. Remove from heat and stir in lime juice when cool.

These tiny dried fish are found in packets sometimes labelled 'Silver Fish' or 'Ikan Bilis'.

Dried Sprats

Fry in oil for a crisp texture. Serve as accompaniment with rice and curries or as a savoury nibble with drinks.

Chilli Shrimp and Water Chestnuts

Serves 4

- *4 tablespoons dried shrimps*
- *125 g (4 oz) canned bamboo shoot*
- *125 g (4 oz) water chestnuts*
- *60 g (2 oz) bean starch noodles*
- *2 teaspoons dark soy sauce*
- *salt to taste*
- *1 teaspoon sugar*
- *½ cup chicken stock*
- *2 teaspoons chilli sauce*
- *1 teaspoon cornflour*
- *2 tablespoons peanut oil*
- *1 small clove garlic, finely chopped*
- *½ teaspoon finely chopped fresh ginger*
- *½ teaspoon oriental sesame oil*
- *2 tablespoons chopped spring onions*

Soak shrimps in hot water for 30 minutes. Drain well and dry on paper towels. Pulverise in blender and set aside. Chop bamboo shoot and water chestnuts. Bring pan of water to the boil, drop in noodles and boil for 15 minutes. Drain in colander. In a bowl mix soy sauce, salt, sugar, chicken stock, chilli sauce and cornflour.

Heat a wok, add peanut oil and swirl. Add garlic, ginger, pulverised shrimp, bamboo shoot and water chestnuts. Stir-fry for 1 minute. Add soy sauce mixture and stir until it boils and thickens. Stir in sesame oil. Place drained noodles on a serving dish and spoon shrimp mixture on top. Garnish with spring onions and serve immediately.

Served as an accompaniment to curries and rice. The dried shrimps used in this instance are tiny and still in their very thin shells.

Shrimp and Coconut Sambol

Serves 6

- *2 small onions*
- *1 fresh red chilli*
- *1 teaspoon fenugreek seeds*
- *½ teaspoon ground turmeric*
- *½ cup dried shrimps*
- *salt to taste*
- *2½ cups fresh grated coconut or 1½ cups desiccated coconut*
- *2 tablespoons peanut oil*
- *1 sprig fresh curry leaves or 10 dried curry leaves*
- *4 large dried chillies*

Finely slice one of the onions and reserve. Finely chop the other and put in a saucepan with red chilli, fenugreek seeds, turmeric, dried shrimps and ¾ cup water. Bring to the boil and cook for 10 minutes, or until onion is cooked. Taste and add salt if necessary. Add coconut and toss until moisture is absorbed.

In a wok or frying pan heat oil and fry reserved sliced onion, curry leaves and dried chillies. Remove chillies and set aside once they darken. Continue frying onion until dark brown. Add coconut mixture to pan and toss. Mixture should be moist but no liquid should show in pan. Mix in reserved fried chillies and transfer to a serving bowl.

A Sri Lankan favourite, also prepared in Malaysia.

Salt Fish and Eggplant Curry

Serves 6

- *250 g (8 oz) dried, salted fish*
- *500 g (1 lb) eggplants*
- *1 teaspoon ground turmeric*
- *salt to taste*
- *10 large mild chillies*
- *peanut oil for frying*
- *1 large onion, sliced finely*
- *10 cloves garlic, peeled and left whole*
- *1½ cups canned coconut milk*
- *3 tablespoons Ceylon Curry Powder (see p. 84)*
- *small stick cinnamon*
- *1 sprig fresh curry leaves or 8 dried leaves*
- *¼ cup malt vinegar*
- *1 tablespoon dried tamarind pulp*
- *2 teaspoons sugar*

Rinse dried fish, drain, then cut into 5 cm (2 inch) pieces. Cut eggplants into thick slices and rub with turmeric and salt. Leave to drain in a colander for 30 minutes, then dry each slice on paper towels. Slit chillies and discard seeds.

Heat about ¼ cup oil in a frying pan and fry separately dried fish, chillies, onion, garlic and eggplant, transferring each to a dish as it is fried. The eggplant will absorb oil and it might be necessary to add more. Put coconut milk into a large saucepan with curry powder, cinnamon, curry leaves and vinegar. Dissolve tamarind in 1½ cups water and add to pan. Bring to the boil, stirring constantly, then add fried ingredients and cook uncovered until thick. Stir frequently and just before serving stir in sugar.

This is not a bird, but a variety of fish. Don't be put off by its pungent smell, for this crisp and salty dried fish is delicious when eaten in small amounts with rice. You will find it in packets in Asian food stores.

Bombay Duck

Cut into pieces and deep-fry for 1 to 2 minutes in hot oil until golden brown.

Fried Bombay Duck with Chilli

Serves 4

- *6 Bombay Ducks (see above)*
- *½ cup peanut oil*
- *2 medium onions, sliced finely*
- *2 cloves garlic, chopped finely*
- *3 large dried chillies, seeded and broken into pieces*
- *lime juice*

Cut Bombay ducks into 5 cm (2 inch) lengths. Heat oil in a small pan and briefly deep-fry. Remove and drain. Pour off half the oil and in remainder fry onions and garlic over low heat, stirring frequently, until onion is soft and golden. Add chillies and fry for 3 minutes more. Return Bombay duck pieces to pan and stir-fry to mix. Add lime juice to taste. Serve hot or at room temperature.

Accompaniments and Spice Mixes

This is the Chinese method for steaming rice. When cooked, the grains are well defined and separate but still cling together, which makes for easy eating with chopsticks.

Steamed White Rice

Serves 4 to 6

- *2½ cups (500 g) short or medium grain rice*
- *3 cups water*

Wash rice if necessary and drain well. Pour 3 cups of water into a saucepan, add rice and stir. Bring to the boil over high heat and boil rapidly for 1 to 2 minutes. Reduce heat to medium and continue cooking until holes appear in mass of rice and surface looks dimpled. Cover pan with a tight-fitting lid (or place a layer of foil between lid and pan), reduce heat to minimum and continue cooking over very low heat for 10 minutes. Turn off heat and leave rice to sit undisturbed for a further 10 minutes. Do not remove lid during this time.

Note Long grain rice is preferred for Indian dishes and gives a drier, more fluffy result. To cook 500 g long grain rice by this method, increase the amount of water to 3½ cups, as long grain rice has greater absorbency. At the end of cooking time fluff up the rice grains with a fork.

Fried Rice with Seafood

Serves 4

- *250 g (8 oz) small squid*
- *250 g (8 oz) small cooked prawns*
- *1 or 2 Chinese sausages (lap cheong)*
- *1 small red capsicum*
- *2 tablespoons peanut oil*
- *2 teaspoons finely chopped ginger*
- *4 cups cold cooked rice*
- *½ cup frozen peas*
- *2 tablespoons light soy sauce*
- *6 spring onions, sliced diagonally*

Clean squid and cut across into rings. Shell prawns. Steam sausage for 10 minutes, then cut into thin diagonal slices. Cut capsicum into small squares.

Heat oil in a wok and fry ginger until golden. Add squid, capsicum, sausage and prawns and toss briefly, until squid is just cooked. Add rice and peas and stir-fry until grains are separate and lightly coloured. Sprinkle with sauce and toss until evenly mixed. Add spring onions and toss over heat for 1 minute more. Serve hot.

Thai Curry Pastes

Red Curry Paste

Makes about 1 cup

- *4–6 dried red chillies*
- *2 small brown onions, chopped*
- *1 teaspoon black peppercorns*
- *2 teaspoons ground cummin*
- *1 tablespoon ground coriander*
- *2 tablespoons chopped fresh coriander roots*
- *1 teaspoon salt*
- *1 stem lemon grass, sliced finely or 2 teaspoons chopped lemon rind*
- *2 slices galangal in brine*
- *1 tablespoon chopped garlic*
- *2 teaspoons dried shrimp paste*
- *1 teaspoon turmeric*
- *2 teaspoons paprika (see Note)*

Remove stems and seeds from chillies and soak in just enough water to cover for 10 minutes. Purée in a blender with remaining ingredients. Store in a glass jar and refrigerate.

Note I have added paprika for the colour without too much heat.

Green Curry Paste

Makes about 1 cup

- *4 large or 8 small green chillies*
- *1 medium onion, chopped*
- *1 tablespoon chopped garlic*
- *½ cup chopped fresh coriander, including roots, stems and leaves*
- *¼ cup finely sliced lemon grass, or thinly peeled rind of 1 lemon*
- *1 tablespoon chopped galangal in brine*
- *2 teaspoons ground coriander*
- *1 teaspoon ground cummin*
- *1 teaspoon black peppercorns*
- *1 teaspoon ground turmeric*
- *1 teaspoon dried shrimp paste*

Blend and store as for Red Curry Paste.

Ceylon Curry Powder

Makes about 1½ cups

- *1 cup coriander seeds*
- *½ cup cummin seeds*
- *2 tablespoons fennel seeds*
- *1 teaspoon fenugreek seeds*
- *1 x 5 cm (2 inches) cinnamon stick*
- *1 teaspoon whole cloves*
- *1 teaspoon cardamom seeds*
- *2 tablespoons dried curry leaves*
- *2 teaspoons chilli powder, optional*
- *2 tablespoons ground rice, optional*

Roast first 4 seeds separately in a dry pan over low heat, stirring, until dark brown. Blend on high speed with cinnamon, cloves, cardamom and curry leaves until finely ground. Mix with chilli powder and ground rice if used. Store airtight.

Garam Masala

Makes about ½ cup

- *4 tablespoons coriander seeds*
- *2 tablespoons cummin seeds*
- *1 tablespoon whole black peppercorns*
- *2 teaspoons cardamom seeds (measure after roasting and removing from pods)*
- *4 x 7.5 cm (3 inch) cinnamon sticks*
- *1 teaspoon whole cloves*
- *1 whole nutmeg*

Roast each spice separately in a small, heavy-based pan. Turn each one out onto a plate to cool as soon as it smells fragrant. Discard pods from roasted cardamom, using only seeds. Blend spices except nutmeg to a fine powder. Finely grate nutmeg and mix in. Store airtight.

Glossary

You can find most of these ingredients in Asian food stores, but many are sold in supermarkets, etc.

Banana leaves Fresh banana leaves are used for wrapping food before cooking. Banana leaves impart a delicate flavour to food. Available in Asian shops, but foil can be substituted.

Basmati rice A fragrant rice with fine, long grains. Sold in Indian grocers and some supermarkets. Easy to cook but requires washing. Leave at least 30 minutes in colander to drain and dry.

Bean thread vermicelli Made from mung beans, these noodles are fine and transparent.

Bird's eye chillies Small, very hot chillies used in South-East Asian food.

Black beans Salted, fermented soy beans are sold in packets or cans. Very salty, so rinse before use.

Bonito A dark, oily fish with smooth, silver-grey skin.

Chillies Fresh or dried chillies are an essential ingredient in Asian cooking. Wear gloves when handling them and don't touch your eyes or face with hands that might have even the slightest trace of chilli.

Chinese broccoli (gai larn) A dark green vegetable with white flowers, used mostly for its stems.

Chinese sausage (lap cheong) There are two types, one made from lean and fat pork, the other containing some liver. Use the former, which is a light red in colour, rather than the latter, which is dark. They keep for weeks in the refrigerator. Steam for at least 10 minutes before using.

Choy sum One of the many green vegetables loosely called Chinese cabbage. Prized for its leaves and stems.

Coriander The fresh herb and the dried seed are used in Asian cooking. When making Thai curry pastes look for fresh coriander with the roots intact.

Curry leaves Increasingly available fresh, these leaves of *murraya koenigii* are essential in South Indian food. Instead of a sprig of fresh leaves, you can use about a dozen dried ones.

Fenugreek Small, flat, pale brown seeds with a slightly bitter flavour, so use with discretion. An essential component of commercial curry powders.

Fish sauce A thin, pale-coloured, very salty sauce made by salting fish and leaving to ferment. Very popular in the cuisines of South-East Asia.

Galangal, greater (laos, lengkuas and kha) An aromatic rhizome, *Alpinia galanga*, similar in size and appearance to ginger but with different flavour. Sold in large slices bottled in brine. Keeps indefinitely in the refrigerator. Also sold as dried slices or powder.

Galangal, lesser (aromatic ginger, kencur, zeodary or krachai) (*Alpinia officinarum*) Smaller in size but stronger in flavour, it is used less often than greater galangal. Sold bottled in brine in fine strips, or dried and powdered.

Ginger A very important rhizome in Asian seafood cookery, especially among the Chinese, who rely on ginger to remove the fishy taste.

Hoi Sin sauce A thick, sweet and spicy sauce used in Chinese dishes. Sold in jars, it keeps indefinitely without refrigeration.

Hot radish, bottled (chilli radish) A good way to give zing to a dish. Use sparingly as it is pungent.

Kaffir lime leaves Fragrant leaves of a special variety of citrus. These are worth searching for and in many capital cities they are sold fresh. Next best thing is frozen or dried leaves, although these are too tough to eat and can only be used in a soup or curry to impart flavour.

Laksa leaves (Vietnamese or Cambodian mint) So-called in Singapore and Malaysia because the leaves are an integral part of the famous fish soup, Laksa. They are hot, adding wonderful flavour and are not mint at all, but *polygonum odoratum*. Ask for the plant by any of its names at good nurseries. It strikes easily in water and, if planted in a sunny spot and watered copiously, will grow in most temperate and tropical climates.

Laos root See **Galangal, greater**.

Lemon grass A fragrant herb which can be simmered whole in a dish. When it is to be ground with other spices, however, it must first be thinly sliced as it is quite fibrous.

Lily buds These exotic-sounding dried tiger lily buds have little flavour, but I am assured that they have nutritional value.

Mushrooms, dried The mushrooms used in this book are the variety known as shiitake and commonly called Chinese mushrooms, though they are common to Japanese and Korean food also. Do not substitute dried European mushrooms: the flavour is totally different.

Mustard cabbage (gai choy) A tangy Chinese vegetable with bright green, ridged stems.

Okra Slightly furry, green pods containing small, white seeds. Sweet and delicately flavoured, its most prominent feature is a mucilaginous texture which some people can't abide. Used in Cajun cooking to give texture to gumbo. Also very popular in Asian dishes.

Oriental sesame oil Buy at Chinese groceries—the roasting of the sesame seeds gives a wonderful flavour to the oil. Sesame oil sold at health food shops is pale and lacks this flavour.

Pandan The Malay or Indonesian name for *pandanus latifolia*, the leaves of which are used to flavour food.

Red ginger Knobs of ginger preserved in a sweet and slightly salty deep red syrup. Finely sliced or shredded, they make a good addition to sauces for fish.

Rice wine (mirin) Used in Japanese food. Substitute dry or sweet sherry.

Sambal ulek (oelek, olek) Fresh chillies ground with salt and sold in jars. An easy way to get the flavour and heat of chillies.

Shrimp paste Dried shrimp paste is a pungent ingredient used in small quantities in South-East Asian food. Sold in blocks or jars and lasting indefinitely, it brings out flavour in Asian food, much as anchovy sauce or anchovy paste does in Western food.

Wasabi (green horseradish) A pungent root used in Japanese food. It has much the same effect as hot English mustard. Sold in powder or paste form, it is now not only found in Japanese shops, but almost every decent-sized fish market, as it is essential as a dip for sashimi or other raw fish dishes. No substitute.

White poppy seeds Use in Indian dishes to thicken sauces, or substitute ground almonds. Buy in small quantities and store in your freezer as they can go rancid.

White radish Very large, shaped like a giant carrot, this is called daikon in Japanese and lo bok in Cantonese. Shredded and soaked in iced water, it becomes mild, sweet and crunchy.

Index